EARLIER AMERICAN MUSIC
EDITED BY H. WILEY HITCHCOCK
for the *Music Library Association*

19

HENRY CLAY WORK

SONGS

HENRY CLAY WORK

SONGS

INTRODUCTION BY H. WILEY HITCHCOCK

Director, Institute for Studies in American Music,
Brooklyn College, CUNY

DA CAPO PRESS • NEW YORK • 1974

Library of Congress Cataloging in Publication Data

Work, Henry Clay, 1832-1884.
    Songs.

    (Earlier American music, 19)
    "This Da Capo Press edition of Songs of Henry Clay
Work is an unabridged republication of the original
volume, published in New York (c. 1884)."
    1. Songs with piano. 2. United States—History—
Civil War, 1861-1865—Songs and music. I. Series.
M1620.W897S6   784.6′8′9737   73-5099
ISBN 0-306-70586-9

This Da Capo Press edition of *Songs of Henry Clay Work* is an unabridged
republication of the original volume, published in New York (*c.* 1884).

Library of Congress Catalog Card Number 73-5099
ISBN 0-306-70586-9

Copyright © 1974 by the Music Library Association

Published by Da Capo Press, Inc.
A Subsidiary of Plenum Publishing Corporation
227 West 17th Street, New York, N.Y. 10011

All Rights Reserved

Manufactured in the United States of America

EDITOR'S FOREWORD

American musical culture, from Colonial and Federal Era days on, has been reflected in an astonishing production of printed music of all kinds: by 1820, for instance, more than fifteen thousand musical publications had issued from American presses. Fads, fashions, and tastes have changed so rapidly in our history, however, that comparatively little earlier American music has remained in print. On the other hand, the past few decades have seen an explosion of interest in earlier American culture, including earlier American music. College and university courses in American civilization and American music have proliferated; recording companies have found a surprising response to earlier American composers and their music; a wave of interest in folk and popular music of past eras has opened up byways of musical experience unimagined only a short time ago.

It seems an opportune moment, therefore, to make available for study and enjoyment— and as an aid to furthering performance of earlier American music—works of significance that exist today only in a few scattered copies of publications long out of print, and works that may be well known only in later editions or arrangements having little relationship to the original compositions.

Earlier American Music is planned around several types of musical scores to be reprinted from early editions of the eighteenth, nineteenth, and early twentieth centuries. The categories are as follows:

> Songs and other solo vocal music
> Choral music and part-songs
> Solo keyboard music
> Chamber music
> Orchestral music and concertos
> Dance music and marches for band
> Theater music

The idea of *Earlier American Music* originated in a paper read before the Music Library Association in February, 1968, and published under the title "A Monumenta Americana?" in the Association's journal, *Notes* (September, 1968). It seems most appropriate, therefore, for the Music Library Association to sponsor this series. We hope *Earlier American Music* will stimulate further study and performance of musical Americana.

H. Wiley Hitchcock

INTRODUCTION

Son of Alanson Work, anti-slavery advocate imprisoned for aiding runaway slaves seeking freedom on the Underground Railroad, Henry Clay Work (1832-1884) was one of the three major song composers of the Civil War era (the others were Stephen Foster and George Frederick Root). Not prolific, Work composed only some seventy-five songs over the thirty-year period between 1853 and 1884. Nevertheless, a good proportion of these were incredibly popular in their time, a few are still well-known today, and all exemplify the nineteenth-century American passion for homely songs of topicality and sentiment.

Self-taught in music, Work got his start (as did his contemporary, Foster) with help from the famous minstrel E. P. Christy, who in 1853 lent his name to Work's first publication, *We Are Coming, Sister Mary,* "arranged and adapted by E. P. Christy and sung at Christy's American Opera House." But it was only after the outbreak of the war, by which time he was associated with the enterprising Chicago music publishers, Root & Cady, that Work began to write in earnest. About half of his songs were published between 1861 and 1867. He then became inactive, producing only fitfully until 1876-77, when in a burst of activity he wrote thirteen songs. Fallow years followed until 1882-83, when his last songs were issued.

Work's first big hit was aided by the kind of commercial promotion that would become commonplace in the twentieth century but was a new American phenomenon in the mid-nineteenth. For a solid week in April 1862, street posters and newspaper advertisements cryptically proclaimed: "Kingdom Coming!" On April 23rd, Christy's Minstrels opened a new show with that title, which had come from a new song by Work. *Kingdom Coming* became an instant success: 8,000 copies were sold within three months; by November, sales had passed 20,000; in less than a year the rallying song was reported as being sung even by slaves behind the Confederate lines.

The following year Work tried to match the success of *Kingdom Coming* with a sequel, *Babylon is Fallen,* but it did not catch on. Two years later, however, Work produced *Marching Through Georgia,* a jaunty valedictory to the war that soon was on everyone's lips and even threatened the all-time Civil War favorites, *Tramp! Tramp! Tramp!* and *The Battle Cry of Freedom* (both by Work's associate George Root).

Besides those on Civil War subjects, Work wrote songs that mirror the thoughts and fancies of his day. Some were for minstrel shows (such as the very popular *Wake Nicodemus!*), others for the parlor. Some are story-telling ballads, others tear-jerking monologues. Of the latter, best-known and longest-lived is *Come Home, Father!* (1864); even today, its first line ("Father, dear father, come home with me now") conjures up images of the temperance melodramas in which it found a place. (It too was initially a manufactured hit: Root & Cady offered a free copy of the sheet music to anyone who could read the lyrics without weeping; of the estimated 10,000 readers of their house organ, *The Song Messenger,* only ten dry-eyed stoics could claim copies.)

After the Civil War, during his period of inactivity and personal obscurity, Work produced only one truly successful song, *Grandfather's Clock* (1876), which sold hundreds of thousands of copies. When he died in 1884, many were surprised to learn that he had not died long before. We owe the present volume of thirty-nine songs to his nephew, Bertram G. Work, who had it privately printed in a facsimile edition shortly after Work's death. (Thus this Da Capo edition is a reprint of a reprint.) Bertram's adulatory preface should be read with caution.*

H.\v.H.

*Its biographical misstatements have been corrected by Richard S. Hill in an article both amusing and touching: "The Mysterious Chord of Henry Clay Work," *Notes,* X (1953), 211-25, 367-90; the same article gives a complete list of Work's compositions with their dates. I should like also to record my indebtedness to another study bearing on Work's career, Dena Epstein's *Music Publishing in Chicago Before 1871: The Firm of Root & Cady, 1858-1871* (Detroit, 1969).

Henry Clay Work

SONGS

SONGS

OF

HENRY CLAY WORK

✓ ✓ ✓ ✓ ✓ ✓

POET AND COMPOSER

BORN 1832   DIED 1884

✓ ✓ ✓ ✓ ✓ ✓

*Compiled by Bertram G. Work, nephew of the
author, and presented with his compliments*

Bring the good old bugle boys!
We will sing another song —
Sing it with a spirit that will start
the world along —
Sing it as we used to sing it
fifty thousand strong,
While we were marching through Georgia.

Hurrah! Hurrah! we bring the Jubilee,
Hurrah, the Jubilee.

PRESS OF J. J. LITTLE & IVES CO., NEW YORK

HENRY CLAY WORK

KNOW the songs of a country, and you will know its history; for the true feeling of a people speaks through what they sing. During a period of great stress, the popular songs of the day invariably give the most accurate expression of the popular mind. What the people of the North thought and felt before and during the Civil War is clearly mirrored by the song writers of the period, among whom the name of Henry Clay Work leads all the rest.

He is often termed the War Poet. Author of "Marching Through Georgia," he would, had he written no other song, have due claim to the title. In addition, he wrote the "Song of a Thousand Years," and many another famous war song. The melody and verse of Henry Clay Work, however, reveal more than the national history of the Civil War. They picture, they record the life of America as it was changing from the last pioneer days into the present great industrial era.

HENRY CLAY WORK was born in Middletown, Connecticut, October 1, 1832, the son of Alanson Work. The family, of Scotch descent, came from Auld Wark Castle. Even in those early days Alan Work was a noted and fearless anti-slavery advocate. When Henry Work was about three years old, his father took the family to Quincy, Illinois, in order to further his welfare work for the slaves. While in Illinois and Missouri, he helped nearly 4,000 slaves to reach freedom by means of the "Underground Railroad." Martyr to the cause he championed, he was imprisoned. For his self-sacrifice, he was warmly praised in a letter sent him by a rising young lawyer of that time—Abraham Lincoln. While in prison, he wrote a book on his anti-slavery experiences. It had a wide sale.

On his release, he returned to Middletown, and subsequently to Hartford, where, as one of the thirteen abolitionist voters in that town, he printed and sold anti-slavery publications. Alanson Work lived till 1879, long enough to see his anti-slavery dream realized, as well as the growing fame of his son.

THAT Henry Clay Work drew much of the inspiration for his songs from his youthful experiences can not be doubted. During his most impressionable years, he came in contact with many noted anti-slavery workers; perhaps even assisted his father in his humanitarian work. A fearless, resourceful boy of eight or ten years may be useful in a cause. Furthermore, the runaway darkies must have been familiar to him from the time he was three years old. In keeping with their natural dramatic instincts as entertainers, they must have amused the child with stories and songs of plantation life while they were hiding in the Work station of the Underground Railroad.

These childish associations and experiences left their imprint on the boy's sensitive mind, and unquestionably called forth such ballads as *Wake Nicodemus*, and *Babylon is Fallen*. His close contact with the negroes accounts for the faithfulness of the dialect of his negro melodies which have so strong an appeal to the darkies themselves.

Henry Clay Work received a common school education in Middletown and Hartford. It was, however, in the printing establishment of Elihu Greer that his talent was developed. While a printer's apprentice he began writing verse, some of which was published at the time in the Hartford newspapers. In a room over the printing shop he found an old melodeon. On this instrument he studied harmony, and composed his first songs, singing them to his friends.

In 1854 Work, a young man, went to Chicago, where he earned his living as a printer. During his spare hours he labored hard at song writing, but with little success. The first song to win him any return was *Coming, Sister Mary*. This he wrote for the Christy Minstrels. His famous temperance ballad, *Father Come Home*, still sung in performances of *Ten Nights in a Bar Room*, was written about this time.

At the very outbreak of the Civil War, Henry Clay Work wrote his first war song, *Kingdom Coming*. He took it to the publishing house of Root & Cady. The head of the company was impressed with the merits of the words as well as the knowledge of harmony shown in the music, and at once offered the young man a contract.

UNTIL the great Chicago fire in 1871, Work continued to write songs for Root & Cady, bringing forth in rapid succession, *Babylon is Fallen*, a sequel to *Kingdom Coming*, *Ring the Bell, Watchman, Song of a Thousand Years*, and *Marching Through Georgia*. Another popular favorite, *Brave Boys are They*, was sung as often in Southern Camps as in Northern. Its appeal caught any soldier.

Work studied harmony in much detail while with Root & Cady, and grew more and more skillful in the nice use of rhythm. About this time he married, and spent the years of 1865–66 in travel. The great Chicago fire brought to a close his relations with Root & Cady, and he returned East, a much saddened man. Two of his children had died during the last years of his residence in Chicago. All of the original plates of the songs he had written were destroyed in the fire.

He first lived in Philadelphia. Then he went to Vineland, New Jersey, where in company with a younger brother and an uncle, he purchased one hundred and fifty acres of land for speculative purposes. The venture was not a success.

ALL of his time, however, was not spent in business affairs. While at Vineland he wrote *The Upshot Family*, which he published himself. This quaint little volume contains a list of forty-three songs written by him. This list is authoritative, for he published it under his signature. The song, *Lilly Dale*, generally accredited to him in all works of reference, is not mentioned in it. Since nobody else has laid claim to the song, though several versions of the melody have been arranged by authors who have been given full credit for the music, it may be assumed that he wrote the words. In the list is a certain No. 36 concerning which, the author makes this quaint remark, "Though on an unimpeachable subject, has been stricken from the list." It would be interesting to know the theme of the nameless, exiled ballad. The songs listed by Henry Clay Work in *The Upshot Family* are:

1. *We Are Coming, Sister Mary*; 2. *Lilly-Willy-Woken*; 3. *Lost on the Lady Elgin*; 4. *Brave Boys are They*; 5. *Little Hallie*; 6. *Nellie Lost and Found*; 7. *Our Captain's Last Words*; 8. *Beautiful Rose*; 9. *The Girls at Home*; 10. *Kingdom Coming*; 11. *Uncle Joe's Hail Columbia*; 12. *The First Love Dream*; 13. *Grafted Into the Army*; 14. *We'll Go Down Ourselves*; 15. *God Save the Nation*; 16. *Days When We Were Young*; 17. *Little Major*; 18. *Watching for Pa*; 19. *Grandfather Told Me So*; 20. *Song of a Thousand Years*; 21. *Babylon is Fallen*; 22. *Sleeping for the Flag*; 23. *Corporal Schnapps*; 24. *Columbia's Guardian Angels*; 25. *Washington and Lincoln*; 26. *Come Home, Father*; 27. *The Picture on the Wall*; 28. *Wake Nicodemus*; 29. *Marching Through Georgia*; 30. *Ring the Bell, Watchman*; 31. *'Tis Finished*; 32. *The Ship That Never Returned*; 33. *Now, Moses*; 34. *Poor Kitty Popcorn*; 35. *Lillie of the Snow-storm*; 36. *Though on an unimpeachable subject, has been stricken from the list*; 37. *Who Shall Rule this American Nation*; 38. *The Evening Star Went Down*; 39. *Dad's a Millionaire*; 40. *Come Back to the Farm*; 41. *Song of the Red Men*; 42. *Last Grand Camping Ground*; 43. *Agnes by the River*.

THE year 1875 found Henry Clay Work back in Chicago with Root & Cady. Here he wrote in rapid succession many songs which brought him in large royalties, and established his position as a foremost writer of popular songs. At this time he published *Grandfather's Clock*. In keeping with his painstaking character, he had laid this song aside for several years, not satisfied with it. It was his custom never to publish a song until he deemed it his best work. In this case, however, his publishers asked for the manuscript and he resurrected it. They at once published it, and sold over 800,000 copies, netting the author $4,000 in royalties.

Notwithstanding the great vogue of his sentimental and pathetic ballads, widely popular in their time, and the enduring, stirring appeal of *Marching. Through Georgia*, Work had a quiet and delicious humor, which gained him quite a following as a writer of humorous songs. *Grafted Into the Army* is a piece whose touches of quiet humor possess great charm. As a bit of satirical writing, *The Upshot Family* has its place in an anthology of true American humor.

WORK'S unassuming disposition kept him from exposing impostors who occasionally laid claim to the authorship of some of his songs. Two such episodes were so amusing that they leave no doubt that Work's sense of humor saved a scene when a humorless individual would have created an uproar.

While visiting a town in Illinois, he attended a concert one evening where a young man sang, *Father, Come Home*, claiming the song as his own. Work sat through the performance smiling, but he made no comment

In 1884 at a Camp Fire Meeting of Minute Men in Brooklyn, a Captain Calhoun was introduced as the author of *Marching Through Georgia*. He sang the song as his own composition. Work's good taste, and a sense of humor saved a bad situation again. The Brooklyn newspapers took up the matter, and after a correspondence with Work's publishers, published the facts of the authorship. Captain Calhoun was heard of no more.

A more serious claim to the authorship of one of Work's songs, because it came long after his death when all possibility of a personal defense had passed, was refuted through the efforts of his friends. In 1902 Mr. A. L. Williams, an employee of the Union Pacific Railroad at Topeka, Kansas, asserted that *Kingdom Coming* was written by a soldier of the 10th Illinois Regiment, under title of *The Contraband*. The New York *Literary Review* published his statement. In controversion of the Williams' claim, evidence of the authorship given by Mr. Root was submitted by Mr. S. Ward Loper of Middletown, Connecticut. It was published, and nothing further was heard from Mr. Williams.

Kingdom Coming was published in 1861 by Root & Cady of Chicago, and later reprinted by other publishers. In every case it was credited to Henry Clay Work.

IN June, 1884, Henry Clay Work went to Hartford to visit his mother, and had been with her but a few days when he died very suddenly from heart trouble. He was buried in Spring Grove Cemetery beside his wife, who had died the year before.

A list of seventy-three songs by Henry Clay Work is possessed by his family, though he doubtless wrote many more. He wrote both the words and music of all of his published pieces, as well as the music for "God Save the Nation," the words of which were written by Theodore Tilton, of the New York *Independent*.

Unlike the fate of many so-called ballads, the songs of Henry Clay Work are still sung throughout America, though they are nearly a half century old. Again, where the fame of song writers usually rests upon a single song, a dozen of Work's songs are equally well known. Of *Marching Through Georgia*, it has well been said, "It is the chief musical legacy of the Civil War."

CONTENTS

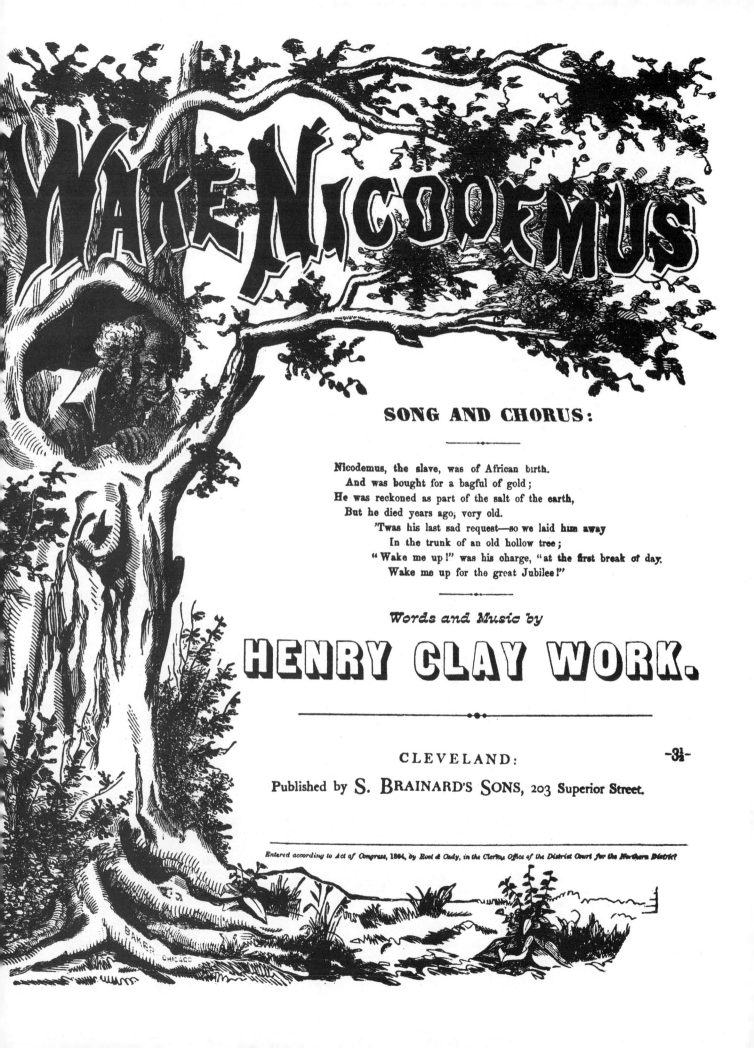

WAKE NICODEMUS

SONG AND CHORUS:

Nicodemus, the slave, was of African birth.
And was bought for a bagful of gold;
He was reckoned as part of the salt of the earth,
But he died years ago; very old.
'Twas his last sad request—so we laid him away
In the trunk of an old hollow tree;
"Wake me up!" was his charge, "at the first break of day.
Wake me up for the great Jubilee!"

Words and Music by

HENRY CLAY WORK.

CLEVELAND:

Published by S. BRAINARD'S SONS, 203 Superior Street.

-3½-

Entered according to Act of Congress, 1864, by Root & Cady, in the Clerks Office of the District Court for the Northern District

Wake Nicodemus!

Words and Music by HENRY C. WORK.
Nº 28

In exact time.

1. Nic - o - de - mus, the slave, was of Af - ri - can birth, And was
2. He was known as a proph-et_ at least was as wise_ For he
3. Nic - o - de - mus was nev - er the sport of the lash, Though the
4. 'Twas a long wea - ry night_ we were al - most in fear That the

bought for a bag - ful of gold; He was reck - on'd as part of the
told of the bat - tles to come; And he trem - bled with dread when he
bul - let has oft cross'd his path: There were none of his mas - ters so
fu - ture was more than he knew; 'Twas a long wea - ry night_ but the

salt of the earth, But he died years a - go, ver - y old. 'Twas his
roll'd up his eyes, And we heed - ed the shake of his thumb. Though he
brave or so rash, As to face such a man in his wrath. Yet his
morn - ing is near, And the words of our proph - et are true. There are

last sad re-quest_ so we laid him a-way In the trunk of an old hol-low
clothed us with fear, yet the gar-ments he wore Were in patch-es at el-bow and
great heart with kind-ness was filled to the brim_ He o-beyed who was born to com-
signs in the sky that the dark-ness is gone_ There are to-kens in end-less ar-

tree. "Wake me up!" was his charge, "at the first break of day_ Wake me
knee; And he still wears the suit that he used to of yore, As he
mand: But he long'd for the morn-ing which then was so dim_ For the
ray; While the storm which had seem-ing-ly ban-ished the dawn, On-ly

Chorus.

AIR

up for the great Ju-bi-lee!" The "Good Time Coming" is al-most here! It was
sleeps in the old hol-low tree.
morn-ing which now is at hand.
hast-ens the ad-vent of day.

ALTO

TENOR

The "Good Time Coming" is al-most here! It was

BASS

long, long, long on the way! Now run and tell E-li - ja to hur-ry up Pomp, And

long, long, long on the way! Now run and tell E-li - ja to hur-ry up Pomp, And

meet us at the gum-tree down in the swamp, To wake Nic - o-de - mus to - day.

meet us at the gum-tree down in the swamp, To wake Nic - o-de - mus to - day.

COMPOSITIONS

OF

Henry C. Work.

CLEVELAND:

Published by S. BRAINARD'S SONS, 203 Superior St.

Entered according to Act of Congress, A. D. 186 by ROOT & CADY, in the Office of the Librarian of Congress, at Washington.

To Mrs. L. A. Chamberlin, Lebanon, N.H.

The Days When We Were Young

Words and Music by HENRY C. WORK.
Nº 16.

1. Sis - ter! Sis - ter! don't you re-mem - ber The
2. Sis - ter! Sis - ter! don't you re-mem - ber The
3. Sis - ter! Sis - ter! don't you re-mem - ber The

days when we ___ were young? _____ The long, long days, with a
days when we ___ were young? _____ The home - ly house in the
days when we ___ were young? _____ The mates of child - hood ___ the

light and a shade Like the pearls of a neck - lace strung _____ Like the
far, far a - way, Where the love of our child - hood clung _____ Where the
friends of our youth ___ We com - pan - ion'd and lov'd a - mong _____ We com -

pearls of a neck - lace strung? They are gone, with all our
love of our child - hood clung? There is naught to mark that
pan - ion'd and lov'd a - mong? Some are wan - d'ring far, and

yes - ter days__ We seek their like in vain; _____ But
sa - cred spot, Save now the beat - en loam; _____ Yet
some in death Have closed their wea - ry eyes; _____ But

we will shed no tears for them While the bright to - days re-
dis - tant al - tars have we rear'd In the bless - ed name of
we re - joice in new found friends, While we weep for bro - ken

main, _____ While the bright to - days re - main.
home, _____ In the bless - ed name of home.
ties, _____ While we weep for bro - ken ties.

To Cousin Mary Lizzie Work,

Of New Washington, Indiana.

SONG AND CHORUS,

In Honor of Maj. Gen. SHERMAN'S FAMOUS MARCH "from Atlanta to the Sea."

Words and Music by

HENRY CLAY WORK.

CLEVELAND:

Published by S. BRAINARD'S SONS, 203 Superior St.

Marching Through Georgia

Words and Music by HENRY C. WORK
Nº 29

Introduction

1. Bring the good old bu - gle, boys! we'll
2. How the dar - keys shout - ed when they
3. Yes, and there were Un - ion men who
4. "Sher - man's dash - ing Yan - kee boys will
5. So we made a thor - ough - fare for

sing an - oth - er song___ Sing it with a spir - it that will
heard the joy - ful sound! How the tur - keys gob - bled which our
wept with joy - ful tears, When they saw the hon - or'd flag they
nev - er reach the coast!" So the sau - cy reb - els said, and
Free - dom and her train, Six - ty miles in la - ti - tude___ three

start the world a- long____ Sing it as we used to sing it
com - mis - sa - ry found! How the sweet po- ta- toes e - ven
had not seen for years; Hard - ly could they be re- strained from
'twas a hand some boast, Had they not for- got, a - las! to
hun - dred to the main; Trea - son fled be - fore us for re -

fif - ty thou - sand strong, While we were march-ing through Geor - gia.
start-ed from the ground, While we were march-ing through Geor - gia.
break-ing forth in cheers, While we were march-ing through Geor - gia.
reck-on with the host, While we were march-ing through Geor - gia.
sis-tance was in vain, While we were march-ing through Geor - gia.

Chorus

AIR

Hur - rah! Hur-rah! we bring the Ju- bi - le! Hur - rah! Hur-rah! the

ALTO

TENOR

Hur - rah! Hur-rah! we bring the Ju- bi - le! Hur - rah! Hur-rah! the

BASS *ff*

Marching Through 3

20

flag that makes you free!" So we sang the cho - rus from At -

flag that makes you free!" So we sang the cho - rus from At -

lan - ta to the sea, While we were marching through Geor - gia.

lan - ta to the sea, While we were marching through Geor - gia.

SONG AND CHORUS.

WORDS AND MUSIC BY

HENRY C. WORK.

3½

CLEVELAND:
PUBLISHED BY S. BRAINARD'S SONS, 203 SUPERIOR STREET.

The Song Of The Red Man

Words and Music by HENRY C. WORK
Vineland, N. J. Nº 41

When the pale - fa - ces came in their white-wing'd ca-noes, Long a - go, from the sun - ris - ing

We re - ceiv'd them with glad - ness, as Sons of the Sky We be - liev'd them of heav - en - ly

When the oaks, pines and ce - dars were fell'd to the ground, 'Twas a sight that with sor - row we

sea
When they ask'd for a lodge, and we did not re-fuse Hap - py

birth;
But a - las! to our sor - row we found by and by, That like

saw;
For the game fled af-fright - ed, and no food was found For the

then was the red man, and free.
He could then choose a spot for his

us they were born of the earth.
By their false trad - ers wrong'd, by their

old chief, the pa - poose and squaw.
Driv - en west - ward we came, but the

wig - wam to stand, Where the for - est was crowd - ed with game; For the

fire - wa - ter craz'd, There was no one our braves to re - strain; So the

pale-face was here, With his sharp axe and death-flash-ing gun; And his

blue - roll - ing lake and the ev - er smil - ing land Were his own till the pale - fa - ces came
swift ar - row flew, and the tom - a-hawk was rais'd While we both morn'd the blood of our slain;
great i - ron horse now is rumbling in the rear O, my brave men! your jour-ney is done.

For the broad grass-y plains and the for-ests deep and grand, Were his own till the pale-fa-ces came.
So the smoke-wreath did cease from the cal-u-met of peace, While we both mourn'd the blood of our slain.
Like the bea - ver and elk like the buf-fa-lo and deer O, my brave men! your jour-ney is done.

Chorus

AIR

They came! they came! like the fierce prai - rie flame, Sweeping on to the sun - set-ting shore:

ALTO

TENOR

They came! they came! like the fierce prai - rie flame, Sweeping on to the sun - set-ting shore:

BASS

Gazing now on its waves, but a hand-ful of braves, We shall join in the chase nev-er-more

Gazing now on its waves, but a hand-ful of braves, We shall join in the chase nev-er-more

Till we camp on the plains where the Great Spir-it reigns, We shall join in the chase nev-er-more.

Till we camp on the plains where the Great Spir-it reigns, We shall join in the chase nev-er-more.

COMPOSITIONS

OF

Henry C. Work.

CLEVELAND:

Published by S. BRAINARD'S SONS, 203 Superior St.

Entered according to Act of Congress, A. D. 186 by ROOT & CADY, in the Office of the Librarian of Congress, at Washington.

Uncle Joe's "Hail Columbia!"

Words and Music by HENRY C. WORK
Nº 11

1. Un - cle Joe comes home a sing - ing, Hail, Co - lum-by!
2. Bressed days, I lib to see dem, Hail, Co - lum-by!
3. Dis is what de war was brought for, Hail, Co - lum-by!

Glorious times de Lord is bring-in'__ Now let me die.
I hab drawn a breff of free-dom__ Now let me die.
Dis is what our fa - ders fought for__ Now let me die.

Maestoso

Chorus

Lord has come to sabe His peo-ple— Now let me die.

Lord has come to sabe His peo-ple— Now let me die.

4. I hab seen de rebels beaten,
    Hail Columby!
I hab seen dar hosts retreatin',—
    Now let me die.
O! dis Union can't be broken,
    Dar's no use to try;
No sech ting de Lord has spoken—
    Now let me die.

CHORUS   Ring de Bells, &c.

5. I'll go home a singing "Glory!"
    Hail Columby!
Since I heard dis bressed story—
    Now let me die.
'Tis de ransom ob de nation,
    Drawin' now so nigh;
'Tis de day ob full salbation,—
    Now let me die.

CHORUS   Ring de Bells, &c.

COMPOSITIONS

OF

Henry C. Work.

CLEVELAND:

Published by S. BRAINARD'S SONS, 203 Superior St.

Entered according to Act of Congress, A. D. 186 by ROOT & CADY, in the Office of the Librarian of Congress, at Washington.

Babylon Is Fallen!

Sequel to "Kingdom Coming"

Words and Music by HENRY C. WORK
Nº 21

1. Don't you see de black clouds   Ris - in' o - ber yon - der,
2. Don't you see de light - nin'   Flash - in' in de cane - brake,
3. Way   up in de corn - field,   Whar you hear de tun - der

Whar de Mas-sa's ole plan-ta-tion am? Neb-ber you be fright-ened
Like as if we gwine to hab a storm? No! you is mis-ta-ken
Dat is our ole for-ty pounder gun? When de shells are miss-in',

Dem is on-ly dar-keys, Come to jine an' fight for Un-cle Sam.
'Tis de dar-key's bay-'nets, An' de but-tons on dar u-ni-form.
Den we load wid punk-ins, All de same to make de cow-ards run.

Chorus

AIR
Look out dar, now! We's a gwine to shoot! Look

ALTO
Look out dar, now! We's a gwine to shoot! Look

TENOR
Look out dar, now! We's a gwine to shoot! Look

BASS

4. Massa was de Kernel
   In de rebel army,
Ebber sence he went an' run away;
   But his lubly darkeys,
   Dey has been a watchin',
An' dey take him pris'ner tudder day.
   Chorus—Look out dar, &c.

5. We will be de massa,
   He will be de sarvant —
Try him how he like it for a spell;
   So we crack de Butt'nuts,
   So we take de Kernel,
So de cannon carry back de shell.
   Chorus—Look out dar, &c.

ROOT & CADY'S
VOCAL
QUARTETTS

With Pianoforte Accompaniment.

For Men's Voices.—1st and 2d Tenor, and 1st and 2d Base.

Forward Boys..*G. F. Root.* 2
Key of C. 3-4 and 2-4 time. First Tenor goes up to A. First movement *andante—second allegro.*

March on ! March on !...Soldier's Glee....................*Wm. Lewis.* 3
Key of B flat. 6-8 time. First Tenor goes up to G. Has a Duet—bold and energetic.

Come on this Silent Night...Serenad... ....*James Grant Wilson.* 1½
Key of A flat. 3-4 time. First Tenor goes up to A flat. Has some modulations. Smooth, flowing.

The Outward Bound...Sailor's Glee........................*J. Molter.* 3
Key of D. 4-4 time. First Tenor goes up to G. Second Base to F sharp below. Has triplets in all the parts—spirited and rather difficult.

Have ye Sharpened your Swords ?...Battle Song...........*Manchester.* 2
Key of G—6-8 time. First Tenor goes up to G. With fire.

For Mixed Voices.—Soprano, Alto, Tenor and Base.

God Save the Nation..................................*Henry C. Work.* 2
Key of G—4-4 time. Not difficult. All the parts within ordinary compass.

Wake, Lady, Wake ! we are Singing to Thee...Serenade......*Root.* 4
Key of G—6-8 time. Solo for Tenor goes up to G. Moderately difficult.

Row, Row, Homeward we go.........................*S. W. Martin.* 3½
Key of F—6-8 time. Barcarolle movement. Within usual compass. Moderately difficult.

God bless our brave young Volunteers...................*Geo. F. Root.* 2
Key of C—3-4 time. Earnest and patriotic.

Girls at Home..*Henry C. Work.* 3
Key of A—4-4 time. Companion to "Brave Boys are They."

Welcome to Spring...................................*J. W. Martin.* 4
Key of A flat—4-4 time. Has a soprano Solo. Is bright and sparkling.

We meet upon the Level...Masonic..................... ...*C. M. Cady.* 2½
Key of C—2-4 time. Within the usual compass. Has a Chorus after each verse.

A Home in the West...................................*J. M. Hubbard.* 4
Key of E flat—6-8 time. "O give me a home in the beautiful West." Moderately difficult.

Homeward now from Toil returning.....................*J. M. Pelton.* 3
Key of G—3-4 time. Solo for the soprano, with accompaniment by the ther voices, in Swiss style.

My Mother's Grave...................................*H. P. Danks.* 2½
Key of A flat—4-4 time. In the ordinary compass. Tender and gentle.

Softly Dream, Sweet Love............................*S. W. Martin.* 4
Key of B flat—3-4 and 6-8 time. First movement *andante;* second, *allegro.* Pleasing and effective.

The Liberty Bird....................................*Geo. F. Root.* 3
Key of F—in chanting style. Goes up to F.

List, the Evening Breeze is Stealing...................*J. M. Hubbard.* 4
Key of B flat—4-4 time. A boat glee. Moderately difficult.

Father's Come Home..................................*S. K. Whiting.* 3
Key of A flat—4-4 time. Goes up to D flat. Sequel to "Come Home, Father."

God Save The Nation

A Battle Hymn

Words by THEODORE TILTON

Music by HENRY C. WORK.
No 15

1. Thou who or-dain-est, for the land's sal-va-tion, Fam-ine and fire, and

2. By the great sign, for-told, of Thine Ap-pear-ing, Com-ing in clouds, while

3. By the brave blood that flow-eth like a riv-er, Hurl Thou a thun-der

4. Slay Thou our foes or turn them to de-ri-sion, Till, through the blood-red

God Save The Nation 2

DEDICATED TO THE "GIRLS AT HOME."

"Sleeping for the Flag"

A Companion Piece to

"BRAVE BOYS ARE THEY."

"And yet—and yet—we cannot forget
That many brave boys must fall."

SONG AND CHORUS.

Words and Music by

HENRY C. WORK.

⟨8⟩

CLEVELAND:

Published by S. BRAINARD'S SONS, 203 Superior St.

Entered according to Act of Congress, A. D., 1863, by Root & Cady, in the Clerk's Office of the District Court for the Northern District of Illinois.

Sleeping For The Flag

Words and Music by HENRY C. WORK.
Nº 22

Rather Slowly

1. When our boys come home in tri-umph, brother, With the lau-rels they shall gain;
2. You who were the first on du-ty, brother, When "to arms" your leader cried —
3. You have cross'd the clouded riv-er, brother, To the mansions of the blest,

When   we go to give them wel-come,   brother,   We shall look for you   in   vain.
You   have left the ranks for - ev- er,   brother,   You have laid your armes   a - side.
"When   the wicked cease from troubling," brother,   "And the wea-ry are   at   rest?"

We   shall wait for your re - turn-ing,   brother,   Though we know it can-not   be;
From   the aw- ful scenes of bat-tle,   brother,   You   were set for-ev- er   free,
Sure - ly we would not re - call you,   brother,   But   the tears flow fast and   free,

For   your comrades left you sleeping,   brother,   Un-der-neath a south - ern   tree.
When   your comrades left you sleeping,   brother,   Un-der-neath that south - ern   tree.
When   we think of you   as sleeping,   brother,   Un-der-neath that south - ern   tree.

Sleeping For The Flag 3

Chorus

COMPOSITIONS

OF

Henry C. Work.

BALLADS.

Days when we were young	30
First Love Dream	30
Our Captain's Last Words	30

SONGS & CHORUSES.

Agnes by the River	30
Andy Veto	30
Babylon is Fallen	30
Beautiful Rose	30
Buckskin Bag of Gold	35
Columbia's Guardian Ang ls	30
Come back to the Farm	30
Come Home Father	30
Corporal Schnapps	30
Grafted into the Army	30
Grandmother told me so	30
Kingdom Coming	30
Lillie of the Snow Storm	30
Little Major	30
Marching through Georgia	30
Nellie Lost and Found	30
Now Moses	30
No Letters from Home	35

Our last grand Camping Ground	30
Picture on the Wall	30
Ring the Bell, Watchman	25
Ship that never returned	30
Sleeping for the Flag	30
Song of a thousand Years	30
Song of the Red Man	35
'Tis Finished	30
Uncle Joe's Hail Columbia	30
Wake Nicodemus,	35
Wake the Boys to search for Nellie	30
Washington and Lincoln	30
Watching for Pa	30
We'll go down Ourselves	30
Who shall Rule this American Nation	30
When the Evening Star went down	30

DUETS.

Sleep Baby, Sleep	30

QUARTETS.

Crossing the Grand Sierras	75
Girls at Home	30
God save the Nation	25
Poor Kitty Pop Corn	35

CLEVELAND:

Published by S. BRAINARD'S SONS, 203 Superior St.

To Mrs. Aurelia A. Work, Hartford, Conn.

Our Captain's Last Words

Words and Music by HENRY C. WORK
Nᵒ 7

1. Where the fore - most flag was fly-ing, Pierc'd by ma - ny a shot and shell,
2. Through the bat - tle smoke they bore him, But his words were grow - ing wild;
3. Men who were not used to weep-ing, Turn'd a - side to hide a tear,

Where the brav - est men were dy-ing, There our gal - lant
Heed - ing not the scenes be-fore him, Ste - phen was once
When they saw the pal - lor creep-ing, That as - sured them

cap - tain fell. "Boys! you fol - low now a - no - ther!
more a-child. "Ah, she comes! there is no o - ther
death was near. Kind - ly as he were a broth - er,

Fol - low till the foe shall yield"; Then he whis - per'd,
Speaks my name with such a joy; Press me to your
Stran - gers caught his part - ing breath, La - den with the

46

"Tell my moth-er Ste-phen died up-on the field."
bo som, moth-er Call me still your dar-ling boy."
mur - mur "moth-er" Last up - on his lips in death.

"Moth-er!"_____ "Moth-er!"_____ Ste - phen died up-
"Moth-er!"_____ "Moth-er!"_____ Call me still your
"Moth-er!"_____ "Moth-er!"_____ Last up - on his

on the field."
dar - ling boy."
lips in death.

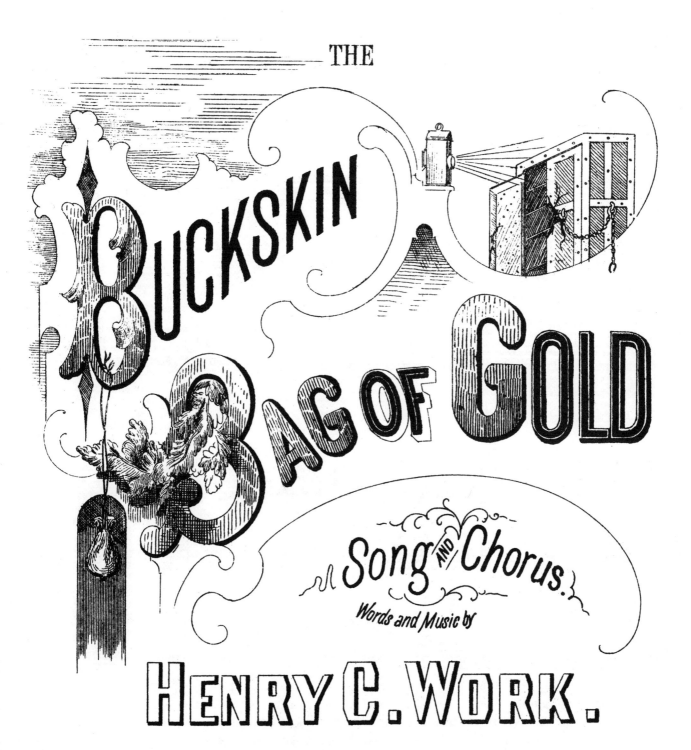

THE

BUCKSKIN BAG OF GOLD

Song AND Chorus.

Words and Music by

HENRY C. WORK.

3½

Published by S. Brainard's Sons Cleveland.

The Buckskin Bag Of Gold

Words and Music by HENRY C. WORK
Nº 45

gave me such a search - ing glance Of sweet - ly charm'd sur - prise! I
I should live a thou - sand years, No oth - er hears my vow. Like
"Grand Ho - tel" he must have stopp'd, I won - der when he came! He
this I read! why, Pa - pa's bank Is robb'd of ev - 'ry cent! The

knew 'twas he the la - dy meant, Who once my for - tune told, By his
Ju - das — no, like Ju - pi - ter, He look'd so brave and bold, With his
must have charm'd those Lump - kin girls, So haugh - ty, proud and cold, By his
thief, it seems, left town last night, Well, well! I'm nice - ly sold! He had

jet black eyes, his grand moustache, And his buck - skin bag of gold.
jet black eyes, his grand moustache, And his buck - skin bag of gold.
jet black eyes, his grand moustache, And his buck - skin bag of gold.
jet black eyes, his grand moustache, And his buck - skin bag of gold.

The Buckskin 4

50

COMPOSITIONS

OF

Henry C. Work.

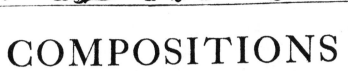

BALLADS.

Days when we were young - -	30
First Love Dream - - - -	30
Our Captain's Last Words - -	30

SONGS & CHORUSES.

Agnes by the River - - -	30
Andy Veto - - - - -	30
Babylon is Fallen - - -	30
Beautiful Rose - - - -	30
Buckskin Bag of Gold - - -	35
Columbia's Guardian Ang ls - -	30
Come back to the Farm - -	30
Come Home Father - - -	30
Corporal Schnapps - - -	30
Grafted into the Army - -	30
Grandmother told me so - -	30
Kingdom Coming - - -	30
Lillie of the Snow Storm - -	30
Little Major - - - -	30
Marching through Georgia - -	30
Nellie Lost and Found - -	30
Now Moses - - - -	30
No Letters from Home - -	35

Our last grand Camping Ground -	30
Picture on the Wall - - -	30
Ring the Bell, Watchman - -	25
Ship that never returned - -	30
Sleeping for the Flag - - -	30
Song of a thousand Years - -	30
Song of the Red Man - - -	35
'Tis Finished - - - -	30
Uncle Joe's Hail Columbia - -	30
Wake Nicodemus, - -	35
Wake the Boys to search for Nellie -	30
Washington and Lincoln - -	30
Watching for Pa - - -	30
We'll go down Ourselves - -	30
Who shall Rule this American Nation	30
When the Evening Star went down -	30

DUETS.

Sleep Baby, Sleep - - -	30

QUARTETS.

Crossing the Grand Sierras - -	75
Girls at Home - - -	30
God save the Nation - - -	25
Poor Kitty Pop Corn - - -	35

CLEVELAND:

Published by S. BRAINARD'S SONS, 203 Superior St.

"Come Home, Father!"

'Tis The

SONG OF LITTLE MARY,

Standing at the bar-room door
While the shameful midnight revel
Rages wildly as before.

Words and Music by HENRY C. WORK
Nº 26

1. Fa-ther, dear fa-ther, come home with me now! The clock in the stee-ple strikes one; You
2. Fa-ther, dear fa-ther, come home with me now! The clock in the stee-ple strikes two; The
3. Fa-ther, dear fa-ther, come home with me now! The clock in the stee-ple strikes three; The

said you were com-ing right home from the shop, As soon as your day's work was done. Our
night has grown cold-er, and Ben-ny is worse But he has been call-ing for you. In
house is so lone-ly the hours are so long For poor weep-ing moth-er and me. Yes,

fire has gone out   our house is all dark   And moth-er's been watch-ing since   tea, ____ With
deed he is worse   Ma says he will die,   Per-haps be-fore morn-ing shall   dawn; ____ And
we are a-lone   poor Ben-ny is dead,   And gone with the an-gels of   light; ____ And

poor brother Ben-ny so   sick in her arms, And   no one to help her but   me. ____ Come
this is the mes-sage she   sent me to bring "Come quick-ly, or   he will be   gone". ____ Come
these were the ver-y last   words that he said   "I   want to kiss Pa-pa good   night". ____ Come

home! come home! come   home! ____ *Please*,   fa-ther, *dear* fa-ther, come   home. ____
home! come home! come   home! ____ *Please*,   fa-ther, *dear* fa-ther, come   home. ____
home! come home! come   home! ____ *Please*,   fa-ther, *dear* fa-ther, come   home. ____

Chorus

Unless each part can be represented, it will be better to omit the Chorus. The Song is complete without it.

AIR

Hear the sweet voice of the child   Which the night winds re-peat as they roam!   Oh

ALTO

TENOR

Hear the sweet voice of the child   Which the night winds re-peat as they roam!   Oh

BASS

who could re-sist this most plain-tive of prayers? "Please, fa-ther, dear fa-ther, come home".

who could re-sist this most plain-tive of prayers? "Please, fa-ther, dear fa-ther, come home".

COMPOSITIONS

OF

Henry C. Work.

CLEVELAND:

Published by S. BRAINARD'S SONS, 203 Superior St.

Entered according to Act of Congress, A. D. 186 by ROOT & CADY, in the Office of the Librarian of Congress, at Washington.

"Watching For Pa."

Words adapted and Music composed by HENRY C. WORK
Nº 18

Introduction

1. Three lit - tle forms in the twi - light gray,
2. May, with her pla - cid and thought - ful brow,
3. Nel lie, with ring - lets of sun - ny hue,
4. Now there are shouts from the win - dow seat

Scan - ning the shad - ows a - cross the way;
Beam - ing with kind - ness and love just now;
Cos - i - ly nest - led be - tween the two;
There is a pat - ter of child - ish feet;

Two pair of black eyes, and one of blue
Wil - lie, the young - est, so ro - guish and gay,
Press - ing her cheek to the win - dow pane,
Gai - ly they rush through the light - ed hall

Brim - ful of love, and of mis - chief too:
Steal - ing sly kiss - es from sis - ter May.
Wish - ing the ab - sent one home a - gain.
"Com - ing at last" is the joy - ful call.

1. 2. 3. Watch - ing for Pa! Watch - ing for Pa!
4. Wel - com - ing Pa! Wel - com - ing Pa!

Sit - ting by the win - dow, Watch - ing for Pa!
Stand - ing on the door - step, Wel - com - ing Pa!

Watching For Pa 3

60

GEMS

—OF—

Western Song.

CLEVELAND:

PUBLISHED BY S. BRAINARD'S SONS, 203 SUPERIOR STREET.

Entered, according to Act of Congress, A. D. 1866, by Root & Cady, in the District Court of
the United States for the Northern District of Illinois

Agnes By The River

Poetry by **MARY J. McDERMIT**

Music by **HENRY C. WORK**

1. Oh! my lit - tle bird, my Ag - nes, with your
2. There is some - thing in the ca - dence that the
3. Sure - ly, ten - der - ness and sad - ness find an

silver sound-ing notes, And your song that tells a sto-ry sad and
words have nev-er told, When by oth-er lips and oth-er voi-ces
ech-o in your heart; And I've heard that hid-den sor-row speak in

sweet; Now your voice is ris-ing soft-ly, and I
sung; And the strain is new in pow-er, though the
song, Mak-ing voi-ces sym-pa-thet-ic, in the

list-en as it floats With the wind that stirs the rip-ples at your feet.
song it-self is old, When it gath-ers life and sweet-ness from your tongue.
u-ni-son with art That is ten-der while it teach-es to be strong.

Agnes By The River 4

64

Chorus

Shin-ing wa-ters quiv-er With the mur-mur of the mu-sic sweet and low.

Shin-ing wa-ters quiv-er With the mur-mur of the mu-sic sweet and low.

4.

Agnes, I have tasted sorrow, and in silence suffered much —

And have learned the art of comforting thereby;

I have sympathy for others, having missed its gentle touch

When my heart was weak and faint enough to die.

5.

That is past! But I am talking as if Agnes heard me now

Yet I've spoken what I meant her not to hear;

And she only heeds the singing of the thrushes on the bough

That is dipping in the sun lit water near.

WORK'S POPULAR SONGS.

NO. 33.

NOW MOSES

SONG AND CHORUS.

WORDS AND MUSIC BY

HENRY C. WORK.

CHICAGO.

CLEVELAND:

Published by S. BRAINARD'S SONS, 203 Superior St.

Entered, according to Act of Congress, A. D. 1865, by Root & Cady, in the Clerk's office of the District Court for the Northern District of Illinois.

"Now, Moses!"

Words and Music by HENRY C. WORK
Nº 33

Impatiently, indignantly and with tears

Now Mo-ses, what makes you so strange and for-get-ful! How is it you heed what I
Now Mo-ses, do tell me now what are you do-ing Off there in the pan-try so
Now Mo-ses, come let us be pleas-ant and clev-er! We must not in fu-ture lead

tell you no more? Just look at your pic-ture—who would not be fret-ful! Your
still and so sly? I know ver-ry well there is some mis-chief brew-ing—Ha!
such a sad life; Come, you be my dear no-ble hus-band for-ev-er, And

great mud-dy boots on my clean kitch-en floor. And there you are smok-ing—Oh
that's what you're af-ter, a whole cher-ry pie. Stop! stop! you are tak-ing the
I'll be for-ev-er your sweet lov-ing wife. Of course, none sup-po-ses that

Here she bursts into tears.

dear, 'tis pro-vok-ing! To tease and tor-ment me it is your de-sire; I'll
last of my bak-ing, The ver-y last pie that was left on the shelf; If
life is all ro-ses, But real-ly I think that—well now I de-clare! You

throw your old—no sir! in-deed I'm not jok-ing—I'll throw your old meer-schaum right
ev-er one did, you de-serve a good shak-ing And I've a great no-tion to
ras-cal! you vil-lain! you stu-pid thing, Mo-ses! You laid your old cur-ry-comb

Chorus

AIR — *Mockingly and ironically.*

in-to the fire! Now Mo-ses, you'll catch it! Now Mo-ses, don't touch it! Now
try it my-self.
right in my chair!

ALTO
Mo - ses! Mo - ses!

TENOR
Mo - ses, you'll catch it! Now Mo - ses don't touch it! Now

BASS
Mo - ses! Mo - ses!

COMPOSITIONS

OF

Henry C. Work.

BALLADS.

Days when we were young - -	30
First Love Dream - - -	30
Our Captain's Last Words - -	30

SONGS & CHORUSES.

Agnes by the River - - -	30
Andy Veto - - - -	30
Babylon is Fallen - - -	30
Beautiful Rose - - - -	30
Buckskin Bag of Gold - - -	35
Columbia's Guardian Ang ls - -	30
Come back to the Farm - -	30
Come Home Father - - -	30
Corporal Schnapps - - -	30
Grafted into the Army - -	30
Grandmother told me so - -	30
Kingdom Coming - - -	30
Lillie of the Snow Storm - -	30
Little Major - - - -	30
Marching through Georgia - -	30
Nellie Lost and Found - -	30
Now Moses - - - -	30
No Letters from Home - -	35

Our last grand Camping Ground -	30
Picture on the Wall - - -	30
Ring the Bell, Watchman - -	25
Ship that never returned - -	30
Sleeping for the Flag - -	30
Song of a thousand Years - -	30
Song of the Red Man - -	35
'Tis Finished - - -	30
Uncle Joe's Hail Columbia - -	30
Wake Nicodemus, -	35
Wake the Boys to search for Nellie -	30
Washington and Lincoln - -	30
Watching for Pa - - -	30
We'll go down Ourselves - -	30
Who shall Rule this American Nation	30
When the Evening Star went down -	30

DUETS.

Sleep Baby, Sleep - - -	30

QUARTETS.

Crossing the Grand Sierras - -	75
Girls at Home - - -	30
God save the Nation - - -	25
Poor Kitty Pop Corn - - -	35

CLEVELAND:

Published by S. BRAINARD'S SONS, 203 Superior St.

Beautiful Rose

Words and Music by HENRY C. WORK.
Nº 8

Off   on the prai-rie,   where the balmy air   Kiss-es the wav-ing   corn,
Rose   is   a   la-dy   yet from early dawn,   La-bors her skill-ful   hand;
Clerks   from the ci-ty,   plow-men from the field,   Lords from a for-eign   land;

There lives a far-mer, with a daughter fair — Fair as a sum-mer's morn!
She is the house-wife, now her mother's gone — Gone to the bet - ter land.
Each in their turn have ver - y humbly kneeled — Kneeled for her heart and hand.

She has a na - ture gen-tle as a dove, Pure as the mountain snows;
Rose has the beau - ty — fa-ther has the gold — Both will be hers one day;
But to them all she made the same re-ply — Kind - ly but firm-ly, "No!"

Say! is it strange that eve-ry-one should love — Love such a girl as Rose?
For she is young, while he is growing old — Old peo-ple pass a - way.
And none but I can tell the reason why — Why she should treat them so.

Beautiful Rose 3

Chorus

2ⁿᵈ time **pp**

AIR

Beau-ti-ful Rose! love - ly Rose! Pride of the prai - rie bower!

ALTO

TENOR

Beau-ti-ful Rose! love - ly Rose! Pride of the prai - rie bower!

BASS

Every-bo-dy loves her__ every-body knows She is the fair-est flower.

Every-bo-dy loves her__ every-body knows She is the fair-est flower.

To Cousin LIZZIE STEWART WOOD, of St. Louis, Mo.

Lillie of the Snowstorm,

—OR—

"PLEASE, FATHER, LET US IN!"

SONG AND CHORUS.

WORDS AND MUSIC BY

HENRY C. WORK.

—3—

CLEVELAND:

Published by S. BRAINARD'S SONS, 203 Superior St.

To cousin Lizzie Stewart Wood, of St. Louis, Mo.

Lillie Of The Snow-Storm

or
"Please, Father, Let Us In!"

Words and Music by HENRY C. WORK

Nº 35

With expression and not too fast

1. To his home, his once-white, once-lov'd cot - tage, Late at night a poor in - e -briate came; To his
2. Far a- cross the prai-rie stood a dwell - ing, Where from harm they oft had found re -treat; Thither
3. Lil-lie prays_the harps are hush'd in Heav - en_ An-gles poise them mid-way in the sky; Up from
4. Morn-ing dawns_the husband and the fa - ther, Sober'd now, to seek his flock has come; Lil-lie

wife, the waiting wife and daugh - ter Who for him had fann'd the midnight flame. Rudely
now, all brave and un-com-plain - ing, Did they urge their wea-ry, way-worn feet. But their
earth there comes a wail of sor - row, Such a wail as must be heard on High. "Fa-ther
dear is liv-ing, but her moth - er—Hours a - go, an an-gel bore her home. Ah, poor

met, they answer'd him with kind - ness—Gave him all their own un-tast-ed store; 'Twas but
strength, un-e-quel to their cour - age, Fail'd them as they wander'd to and fro; Till at
dear! my oth - er bet-ter Fath - er! Won't you hear your daugh-ter Lil-lie pray? Wont you
man! how bit-ter is his an - guish, As he now re-pents his punish'd sin, Bend-ing

small, and he with aw-ful cur - ses, Spurn'd the gift, and drove them from his door.
last, the fee-ble fainting moth - er, Speachless sank up - on the drifted snow.
send some strong and careful an - gel, Who will help my mother on her way?"
o'er the child, who, half un - con - cious, Sad - ly cries, "Please father let us in!"

Chorus

COMPOSITIONS
OF
Henry C. Work.

CLEVELAND:

Published by S. BRAINARD'S SONS, 203 Superior St.

Entered according to Act of Congress, A. D. 186 by Root & Cady, in the Office of the Librarian of Congress, at Washington.

To Miss *ANNA L. BAILEY*
Teacher of Music in the Hyde Park Seminary

The First Love Dream

Words and Music by HENRY C. WORK
Nº 21

1. Last night, moth-er, he told me so, As we walked by the peb - bly
2. Kiss me, moth-er, and share the joy That has on my for - tune
3. Leave you, moth-er, it brings a pang To this light and bound - ing

stream; And I wake so hap-py— so wild with joy, It
smiled; You have shared my sor-rows when e'er I wept, Since
heart; But if he were call-ing, the bride would go, Tho'

seems like a fai - ry dream. But his charm - ing voice is
I was a lit - tle child Do you chide me now? what
you and the daughter part. At a word from him, a

The First Love Dream 3

82

WASHINGTON AND LINCOLN

SONG AND CHORUS:

Words and Music by

HENRY C. WORK.

CLEVELAND:

Published by S. BRAINARD'S SONS, 203 Superior St.

Washington And Lincoln

Words and Music by HENRY C. WORK
Nọ 25

1. Come, hap-py peo - ple! Oh come let us tell   The sto - ry of Washington and Lin - coln!
2. Pa - rents to chil - dren shall tell with de-light, The sto - ry of Washington and Lin - coln;
3. Though on the war   cloud re - cord - ed with steel, The sto - ry of Washington and Lin - coln;

His - to - ry's pa - ges can nev - er ex-cel   The sto - ry of Washington and Lin - coln.
Free born and freed men to - geth - er re cite   The sto - ry of Washington and Lin - coln.
Peace on - ly Peace, can com-plete - ly re-veal   The sto - ry of Washington and Lin - coln.

Down through the a - ges   an an - them shall go,   Bear - ing the hon - ors we glad - ly bestow__
Earth's weary bond men shall lis - ten with cheer__   Ty - rants shall tremble, and trai - tors shall fear__
Thanks to the Lord for the days we be - hold!   Thanks for the un - sul - lied flag we un - fold!

Till ev-ery na - tion and lan- guage shall know The sto - ry of Washington and Lin - coln:
When, in it's full - ness of glo - ry, they hear The sto - ry of Washington and Lin - coln:
Thanks that to us, and in our time, was told The sto - ry of Washington and Lin - coln:

Washington And Lincoln 3

Chorus

Who gave us in-de-pendence, On con-tinent and sea Who saved the glorious Un-ion! And

set a people free! This is the sto-ry__Oh hap-py are we__The sto-ry of Washington and Lin-coln.

Dedicated to MISS LUCY A. PARKER, Greenwich Village, Mass.

LITTLE MAJOR

SONG OR DUETT, WITH CHORUS.

They called him "Little Major,"
The noble drummer boy;
The pride of all his regiment,
And his commander's joy.

WORDS AND MUSIC BY

HENRY C. WORK,

Author of "Kingdom Coming," "Grafted into the Army," etc.

No. 17.  — 3 —

CLEVELAND:

Published by S. BRAINARD'S SONS, 203 Superior St.

Little Major

Words and Music by HENRY C. WORK
Nº 17

1. At his
2. There are

3. Now the
4. See! the

post, the "Lit-tle Ma - jor" Dropp'd his drum, that bat-tle day; On the
none to hear or help him— All his friends were ear-ly fled, Save the

lights are flash-ing round him, And he hears a loy-al word, Strangers
moon that shone a - bove him, Veils her face, as if in grief; And the

grass, all stain'd with crim - son, Through that bat-tle night he lay___ Cry-ing
forms, out streatch'd a - round him, Of the dy - ing and the dead. Hush they

they, whose lips pro - nounce it, Yet he trusts his voice is heard. It is
skies are sad - ly weep - ing___ Shed-ding tear-drops of re - lief. Yet to

"Oh! for love of Je - sus, Grant me but this lit - tle boon! Can you,
come! there falls a foot - step! How it makes his heart re - joice! They will

heard___ Oh, God for - give them! They re - fuse his dy - ing pray'r! "Nothing
die, by friends for - sak - en, With his last re-quest de - nied___ This he

friend, re - fuse me wa - ter? Can you, when I die so soon?"
help, Oh, they will save him, When they hear his faint-ing voice___

but a wound-ed drum - mer," So they say, and leave him there___
felt his keen-est an - guish, When at morn, he gasp'd and died___

Little Major 3

Chorus

AIR

Cry-ing, "Oh! for love of Je - sus, Grant me but this lit - tle boon! Can you,

ALTO

TENOR

Cry-ing, "Oh! for love of Je - sus, Grant me but this lit - tle boon! Can you,

BASS

friend, re - fuse me wa - ter? Can you, when I die so soon?"

friend, re - fuse me wa - ter? Can you, when I die so soon?"

The Ship that Never Return'd.

SONG AND CHORUS.

Words and Music by

HENRY C. WORK.

CLEVELAND:

Published by S. BRAINARD'S SONS, 203 Superior St.

Entered, according to Act of Congress, A.D. 1865, by Root & Cady, in the Clerk's office of the Dist. Court for the Northern Dist. of Illinois.

The Ship That Never Returned

Words and Music by HENRY C. WORK

sum-mer's day, when the wave was rippled By the soft-est, gen-tlest breeze, Did a
fee-ble lad to his anx-ious mother,"I must cross the wide, wide sea; For they
one more trip,"said a gal-lant seaman, As he kiss'd his weep-ing wife; On-ly

ship set sail, with a car - go la-den For a port be-yond the seas; There were

say, perchance in a for - eign climate There is health and strength for me;" 'Twas a

one more bag of the gold - en treasure, And 'twill last us all through life. Then I'll

sweet farewells_there were lov - ing signals, While a form was yet dis - cern'd; Though they

gleam of hope in a maze of dan-ger, And her heart for her youngest yearn'd; Yet she

spend my days in my co - zy cottage, And en - joy the rest I've earn'd; But a-

knew it not, 'twas a sol - emn parting, For the ship she nev-er re - turn'd.

sent him forth with a smile and blessing On the ship that nev-er re - turn'd.

las, poor man! for he sail'd commander Of the ship that nev-er re - turn'd.

94

Chorus

Did she nev-er re - turn? She nev-er re-turn'd Her fate, it is yet un - learn'd; Tho'for

Did she nev-er re-turn? She nev-er re-turn'd Her fate, it is yet un - learn'd; Tho'for

She nev-er re-turn'd Her fate, it is yet un - learn'd; Tho'for

years and years there were fond ones watching, Yet the ship she nev-er re-turn'd.

years and years there were fond ones watching, Yet the ship she nev-er re-turn'd.

years and years there were fond ones watching, Yet the ship she nev-er re-turn'd.

The Ship That Never 3

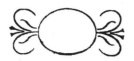

'TIS FINISHED!

OR

SING HALLELUJAH.

Words and Music by

HENRY C. WORK.

③

CLEVELAND:

Published by S. BRAINARD'S SONS, 203 Superior St.

Entered, according to Act of Congress, in the year 1865, by ROOT & CADY, in the Clerk's Office of the District Court, for the Northern District of Illinois.

Tis Finished! or Sing Hallelujah

Words and Music by HENRY C. WORK
No 31

Moderato.

1. 'Tis   fin - ished! 'tis end - ed! The dread and aw - ful task is   done;   Tho'
2. Ye   joy - bells! ye peace bells! Oh nev - er, nev - er mu - sic   rang,   So
3. Come   pat - riots! come free - men! Come join your ev - ery heart and   voice;   We've

wound - ed and bleed - ing, 'tis ours to sing the vic - t'ry won, Our
sweet - ly, so grand - ly, since an - gels in the ad - vent sang, Your
wept with the weep - ing__ now let us with the blest re - joice, With

na - tion is ran - som'd__ our en - e-mies are o - ver - thrown And
mes - sage is glad - ness to myr - i-ads of wait - ing souls, As
ar - mies of vic - tors who round a-bout the white throne stand__ With

now, Now com-men - ces the bright - est e - ra ev - er known.
on - ward and world - ward the hap - py,hap-py ech - o rolls.
Lin - coln, the Mar - tyr and Lib - er-a-tor of his land.

Chorus

Then sing hal - le - lu - jah! sing hal - le - lu - jah! Glo - ry be to God on

Then sing hal - le - lu - jah! sing hal - le - lu - jah! Glo - ry be to God on

Then sing hal - le - lu - jah! sing hal - le - lu - jah! Glo - ry be to God on

high! For the old Flag with the white flag is hang-ing in the a - zure sky.

high! For the old Flag with the white flag is hang-ing in the a - zure sky.

high! For the old Flag with the white flag is hang-ing in the a - zure sky.

Dedicated to THOMAS RICHARDSON CHURCHILL, Boston, Mass.

THE

Picture on the Wall.

SONG & CHORUS.

MUSIC BY

HENRY C. WORK.

CLEVELAND:

Published by S. BRAINARD'S SONS, 203 Superior St.

Dedicated to
THOMAS RICHARDSON CHURCHILL
Boston

The Picture On The Wall

Words adapted and Music composed by HENRY C. WORK
Nº 27

1. 'Tis noon of   night: the sa - ble
2. I hear the   press   of ea - ger
3. The moon's full ra - diance struggles

clouds, Hang weep - ing in the sky; A - lone I sit, where fan-cies flit Like
feet, Up - on my par-lor floor; A moment, and my will-ing arms En -
through, And lights my room once more; And thus shall heav'n O heart of mine, Thy

spec - tral shadows by. Me thinks I see fa - mil-iar forms, And on be-fore them
clasp my boy once more. I feel his warm breath on my cheek, But when his name I
seem - ing loss re - store. Its light shall gild the present gloom, And sweet - er spells en-

all — So fair, so calm, so wondrous like, wondrous like The pic - ture on the wall.
call A shad-owy fin - ger points me to, points me to His pic - ture on the wall.
thral, Than that which binds me to this sweet, to this sweet True pic - ture on the wall.

The Picture On The Wall 3

Chorus

AIR

A - mong the brave and loy - al, How man - y lov'd ones fall!

ALTO

TENOR

A - mong the brave and loy - al, How man - y lov'd ones fall!

BASS

Whose friends be-reft, Have on-ly left, on-ly left A pic - ture on the wall.

Whose friends be-reft, Have on-ly left, A pic - ture on the wall.

The Picture On The Wall 3

WHEN THE EVENING STAR WENT DOWN.

SONG AND CHORUS,

Relating to the loss of the Ocean Steamer "Evening Star" on the morning of October 3d, 1866.

WORDS AND MUSIC BY

HENRY CLAY WORK.

CLEVELAND:

Published by S. BRAINARD'S SONS, 203 Superior St.

When The "Evening Star" Went Down

Words and Music by HENRY C.WORK
Nº 38

1. The morn-ing was fear-ful at sea___ The voy-a-gers wea-ry and pale; Their
2. Sail'd ev-er a ship from her quay, So heav-i-ly la-den as she, With
3. The treacher-ous o-cean is calm___ No lon-ger in storm bil-lows toss'd; Yet

steam-er a wreck, from keel to deck, Be - fore an Au-tum-nal gale. Old
fol-ly and fame, with hope and shame, With van-i - ty, mirth and glee? But
darkness and cloud will long en-shroud The hearts that were link'd with the lost. In

Nep-tune came forth in his power___ He wore on his fea-tures a frown; And
in the dark moment that came, How use-less were rank and re - nown! And
how man-y, how man - y homes, Far dis-tant, in coun-try or town, A

man-y a guest he took to rest, When the "Eve - ning Star" went down.
hon-ors of earth, what were they worth, When the "Eve - ning Star" went down.
light was put out, in dread, in doubt, When the "Eve - ning Star" went down.

When The Evening Star 3

106

Chorus

When The Evening Star 3

To the Hon. LYMAN TRUMBULL, of Chicago.

Who Shall Rule

THIS

American Nation?

SONG AND CHORUS.

WORDS AND MUSIC BY

HENRY C. WORK.

CLEVELAND:

Published by S. BRAINARD'S SONS, 203 Superior St.

To the Hon. Lyman Trumbull.

Who Shall Rule This American Nation?

Words and Music by HENRY C.WORK
Nº 37

1. Who shall rule this A-
2. Who shall rank as the
3. Shall we tar-nish our

mer-i-can Na-tion? Say, boys, say! Who shall sit in the
fam-i-ly roy-al? Say, boys, say! If not those who are
na-tion-al glo-ry? Say, boys, say! Blot one line from the

loft - i - est sta - tion? Say, boys, say! Shall the men who
hon-est and loy - al? Say, boys, say! Then shall one e -
won-der-ful sto - ry? Say, boys, say! Did we vain - ly

tram-pled on the ban - ner? They who now their coun-try would be-tray?
lect-ed as our ser - vant, In his pride, as - sume a re - gal sway?
shed our blood in bat - tle? Did our troops re - sult-less win the day?

They who mur - der the in - no-cent freed-men? Say, boys, say!
Must we bend to the hu-man Dic - ta - tor? Say, boys, say!
Was our time and our treas-ure all squan-der'd? Say, boys, say!

110

Chorus

COME BACK TO THE FARM!

SONG AND CHORUS.

WORDS AND MUSIC BY

HENRY C. WORK.

—3—

CLEVELAND:

Published by S. BRAINARD'S SONS, 203 Superior St.

Come Back To The Farm

Words and Music by HENRY C. WORK
Nº 40

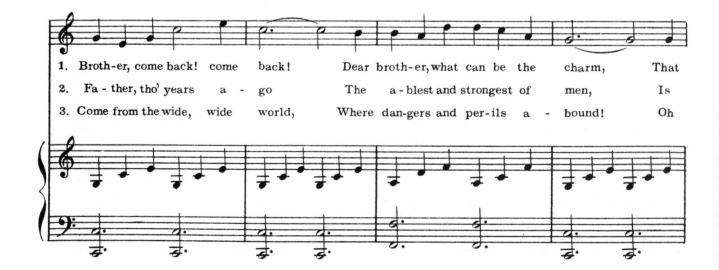

1. Broth-er, come back! come back! Dear broth-er, what can be the charm, That
2. Fa - ther, tho' years a - go The a - blest and strongest of men, Is
3. Come from the wide, wide world, Where dan-gers and per-ils a - bound! Oh

114

Chorus

AIR
'Tis the voice of your sis-ter_she calls you, In tones both of love and a - larm: "By

ALTO
'Tis the voice of your sis-ter_she calls you, In tones both of love and a - larm: "By

TENOR
'Tis the voice of your sis-ter_she calls you, In tones both of love and a - larm: "By

BASS

dead mother's prayers_ by father's gray hairs_Dear broth-er, come back to the farm."

dead mother's prayers_ by father's gray hairs_Dear broth-er, come back to the farm."

dead mother's prayers_ by father's gray hairs_Dear broth-er, come back to the farm."

Come Back To The Farm 3

RING THE BELL, WATCHMAN!

SONG AND CHORUS.

Words and Music by

HENRY CLAY WORK.

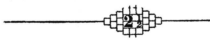

CLEVELAND:

Published by S. BRAINARD'S SONS, 203 Superior St.

Ring The Bell, Watchman

Words and Music by HENRY C. WORK
Nº 30

1. High in the bel-fry the old sex-ton stands, Grasp-ing the rope with his thin bo-ny hands:
2. Bar-ing his long sil-ver locks to the breeze, First for a mo-ment he drops on his knees;
3. Hear! from the hill-top, the first sig-nal gun Thunders the word that some great deed is done;
4. Bon-fires are blaz-ing and rock-ets as-cend___ No mea-gre tri-umph such to-kens portend;

Fix'd is his gaze as by some magic spell, Till he hears the dis-tant murmur, Ring, ring the bell.
Then with a vig-or that few could excel, Answers he the wel-come bidding, Ring, ring the bell.
Hear! thro' the val-ley the long ech-oes swell, Ev-er and a-non re-peat ing, Ring, ring the bell.
Shout, shout! my brothers, for "all, all is well!" 'Tis the u-ni-ver-sal cho-rus, Ring, ring the bell.

Chorus

AIR

"Ring the bell, watchman! ring! ring! ring! Yes, yes! the good news is now on the wing.

ALTO

TENOR

"Ring the bell, watchman! ring! ring! ring! Yes, yes! the good news is now on the wing.

BASS

Yes, yes! they come, and with tid-ings to tell — Glo - ri-ous and blessed tidings — Ring ring the bell!"

Yes, yes! they come, and with tid-ings to tell — Glo - ri-ous and blessed tidings — Ring ring the bell!"

Ring The Bell 2

COMPOSITIONS

OF

Henry C. Work.

BALLADS.

Days when we were young	30
First Love Dream	30
Our Captain's Last Words	30

SONGS & CHORUSES.

Agnes by the River	30
Andy Veto	30
Babylon is Fallen	30
Beautiful Rose	30
Buckskin Bag of Gold	35
Columbia's Guardian Angels	30
Come back to the Farm	30
Come Home Father	30
Corporal Schnapps	30
Grafted into the Army	30
Grandmother told me so	30
Kingdom Coming	30
Lillie of the Snow Storm	30
Little Major	30
Marching through Georgia	30
Nellie Lost and Found	30
Now Moses	30
No Letters from Home	35

Our last grand Camping Ground	30
Picture on the Wall	30
Ring the Bell, Watchman	25
Ship that never returned	30
Sleeping for the Flag	30
Song of a thousand Years	30
Song of the Red Man	35
'Tis Finished	30
Uncle Joe's Hail Columbia	30
Wake Nicodemus	35
Wake the Boys to search for Nellie	30
Washington and Lincoln	30
Watching for Pa	30
We'll go down Ourselves	30
Who shall Rule this American Nation	30
When the Evening Star went down	30

DUETS.

Sleep Baby, Sleep	30

QUARTETS.

Crossing the Grand Sierras	75
Girls at Home	30
God save the Nation	25
Poor Kitty Pop Corn	35

CLEVELAND:

Published by S. BRAINARD'S SONS, 203 Superior St.

Nellie Lost And Found

Words and Music by HENRY C. WORK.
Nº 6

1. Ten o'-clock! the rain be-gins to fall, And Nel-lie still from home!
2. Eleven o'-clock! the lit - tle brothers wait, Still hop-ing her re - turn;
3. Twelve o'-clock! and in the for-est wild, What ter-rors rule the hour!
4. One o'-clock! me - thinks I hear a voice, With ti-dings in its tone!

Vain - ly now, her lov - ing name we call, Oh whither does she roam!
Peep - ing through the lat - tice of the gate, Their dar - ling to dis - cern.
Who can tell what foes surround the child, Or shield her from their power.
Does it bid this trembling heart re-joice, Or sor - row makes it known.

Can it be she wanders from the street, Thro' the wood to find her lone-ly way,
Wea - ry now they turn them to the door, While their tears, for lips that now are dumb,
Storm to face and tor-rents to be cross'd, Beasts of prey that in the dark-ness roam;
Still I hear that mid-night ech-o stirr'd, Sure - ly too, it bears a joy-ful sound;

Bless the child! I fear her lit - tle feet Have car-ried her a - stray.
Ask the ques - tion of - ten asked be-fore, Oh moth-er will she come!
Would to God that on - ly I were lost, And Nel-lie safe at home!
Praise the Lord! a moth-er's pray'r is heard, The dar-ling one is found!

Nellie Lost And Found 3

Chorus

AIR

Wake the boys to search for Nel-lie! Stay not for the dawn;

ALTO

TENOR

(For last verse)
Through the wood the mid-night echoes Bear a joy-ful sound;

BASS

Who shall sleep when from the mother's fold One lit-tle lamb is gone.

Praise the Lord! a moth-er's pray'r is heard, The dar-ling one is found.

Corporal Schnapps

SONG AND CHORUS.

Written and Composed by

HENRY C. WORK.

CLEVELAND:

Published by S. BRAINARD'S SONS, 203 Superior St.

Corporal *Schnapps

Words and Music by HENRY C. WORK.
Nº 23

Not too fast

1. Mine heart ish pro - ken in - to lit - tle pits, I tells you, friend, what for; Mine
2. I march all tay, no mat - ter if der schtorm Pe worse ash Mos - es' flood; I
3. They kives me hart-pread__ tougher as a rock It al - most preaks mine zhaw; I
4. Py'n py we takes von ci - ty in der South We schtays there von whole year; I
5. "Hart times!" you say, "what for you fol - un - teer?" I tolt you, friend, what for: Mine

*"Sch" throughout this song has the soft sound of *sh* as for instance, *Schnapps*

schweetheart, von coot pat - ri - ot - ic kirl, She trives me off mit der war. I
lays all night, mine head up - on a schtump, And "sinks to schleep" in der mud. Der
schplits him some-times mit an i - ron wedge, And cuts him up mit a saw. They
kits me sour krout much as I can eat, And plen - ty loc - car pier. I
schweetheart, von coot pat - ri - ot - ic kirl, She trove me off mit der war. A -

fights for her der pat-tles of te flag I schtrikes so prave as I can; Put
night mare comes I catch him fer - ry pad I treams I schleeps mit der †Ghost; I
kives me peef, so fer - ry, fer - ry salt Like Sod-om's wife, you know; I
meets von la - ty rep-el in der schtreet, So hand-some ef fer I see; I
las! a - las! mine pret-ty lit-tle von Will schmile no more on me; Put

now long time she nix re-mempers me, And coes mit an-oth - er man.
wakes next morn-ing fro-zen in der cround, So schtiff as von schtone post.
sure - ly dinks they put him in der prine Von hun - tred years a - co.
makes to her von fer ry cal lant pow Put ah! she schpits on me.
schtill I fights der pat-tles of te flag To set mine coun-tries free.

*In this line ritard the movement.　　　†Give this note the time of an eighth note only, and rest half a measure.

Corporal Schnapps 3

Chorus

Ah! mine frau-lein! You ish so fer-ry un - kind! You coes mi Hans to

Ah! mine frau-lein! You ish so fer-ry un - kind! You coes mit Hans to

Zher-ma-ny to live, And leaves poor Schnapps pe-hind ___ Leaves poor Schnapps pe-hind.

Zher-ma-ny to live, And leaves poor Schnapps pe-hind Leaves poor Schnapps pe-hind.

ritard - - - -

No Letters from Home!

Song & Chorus.

Words & Music by

Henry C. Work.

— Nº 11 —

3½

Published by S. Brainard's Sons Cleveland.

To
Miss Susie R. Mitchell, Philadelphia

No Letters From Home

Words and Music by HENRY C. WORK
Nº 44

Slowly, distinctly, and with expression

1.
2. Like
3. He
4. "From the

stran-ger lies ill, in a dis-tant cit-y, With no ———— let-ters from
mes-sen-ger doves, from a-cross the moun-tains, Cream tint-ed and gold-en and
moans in his slum-ber "Why did I ev-er So far ———— west-ward-ly
'Gold-en Gate' up to the por-tals pearl-y," He mur-murs, "Oh can it be

miss the phy-sic-ian, and bring a let-ter— A flock of kind let-ters from home." __
this time of sick ness, this hour of dan-ger, Not ev-er one let-ter from home! __
there on Lone Mountain, where sands are drift-ing, But first, bring a let-ter from home." __
mes-sen-ger doves are my long sought let-ters My flock of kind let-ters from home." __

Chorus

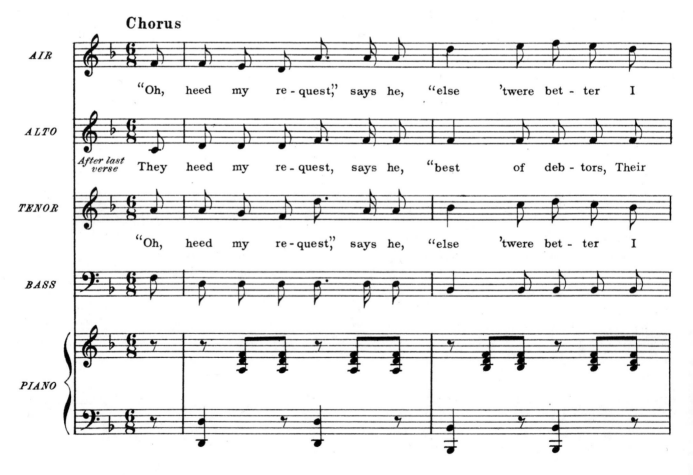

AIR: "Oh, heed my re-quest," says he, "else 'twere bet-ter I

ALTO (*After last verse*): They heed my re-quest, says he, "best of deb-tors, Their

TENOR: "Oh, heed my re-quest," says he, "else 'twere bet-ter I

ROOT & CADY'S
VOCAL
QUARTETTS

With Pianoforte Accompaniment.

For Men's Voices.—1st and 2d Tenor, and 1st and 2d Base.

Forward Boys...*G. F. Root.* 2
Key of C. 3–4 and 2–4 time. First Tenor goes up to A. First movement *andante*—second *allegro.*

March on! March on!...Soldier's Glee........................*Wm. Lewis.* 3
Key of B flat. 6–8 time. First Tenor goes up to G. Has a Duet—bold and energetic.

Come on this Silent Night...Serenad...........*James Grant Wilson.* 1½
Key of A flat. 3–4 time. First Tenor goes up to A flat. Has some modulations. Smooth, flowing.

The Outward Bound...Sailor's Glee...........................*J. Molter.* 3
Key of D. 4–4 time. First Tenor goes up to G. Second Base to F sharp below. Has triplets in all the parts—spirited and rather difficult.

Have ye Sharpened your Swords?...Battle Song...........*Manchester.* 2
Key of G—6–8 time. First Tenor goes up to G. With fire.

For Mixed Voices.—Soprano, Alto, Tenor and Base.

God Save the Nation......................................*Henry C. Work.* 2
Key of G—4–4 time. Not difficult. All the parts within ordinary compass.

Wake, Lady, Wake! we are Singing to Thee...Serenade......*Root.* 4
Key of G—6–8 time. Solo for Tenor goes up to G. Moderately difficult.

Row, Row, Homeward we go..............................*S. W. Martin.* 3½
Key of F—6–8 time. Barcarolle movement. Within usual compass. Moderately difficult.

God bless our brave young Volunteers..................*Geo. F. Root.* 2
Key of C—3–4 time. Earnest and patriotic.

Girls at Home...*Henry C. Work.* 3
Key of A—4–4 time. Companion to "Brave Boys are They."

Welcome to Spring...*J. W. Martin.* 4
Key of A flat—4–4 time. Has a soprano Solo. Is bright and sparkling.

We meet upon the Level...Masonic.....................*C. M. Cady.* 2½
Key of C—2–4 time. Within the usual compass. Has a Chorus after each verse.

A Home in the West......................................*J. M. Hubbard.* 4
Key of E flat—6–8 time. "O give me a home in the beautiful West." Moderately difficult.

Homeward now from Toil returning.......................*J. M. Pelton.* 3
Key of G—3–4 time. Solo for the soprano, with accompaniment by the other voices, in Swiss style.

My Mother's Grave...*H. P. Danks.* 2½
Key of A flat—4–4 time. In the ordinary compass. Tender and gentle.

Softly Dream, Sweet Love................................*S. W. Martin.* 4
Key of B flat—3–4 and 6–8 time. First movement *andante*; second, *allegro.* Pleasing and effective.

The Liberty Bird....*Geo. F. Root.* 3
Key of F—in chanting style. Goes up to F.

List. the Evening Breeze is Stealing..................*J. M. Hubbard.* 4
Key of B flat—4–4 time. A boat glee. Moderately difficult.

Father's Come Home.......................................*S. K. Whiting.* 3
Key of A flat—4–4 time. Goes up to D flat. Sequel to "Come Home, Father."

The Girls At Home

QUARTETTE

Words and Music by HENRY C. WORK
Nº 9

1. When the day-light fades on the tent-ed field, And the camp-fire cheerful-ly

2. When the shad-ows dance on the can-vas walls, And the camp with mel-o-dy

3. Now the sil-ver rays of a set-ting moon Thro' the lof-ty syc-a-mores

burns, Then the sol - dier's thought, like a car - rier dove, To his

rings, 'Tis the good old song of the Stripes and Stars, That the

creep, And the fires burn low, and the sen - tries watch O'er the

own loved home re - turns; Like a car - rier dove a car - rier dove, And

fire - side cir - cle sings; Of the Stripes and Stars the Stripes and Stars For

arm - ed host a - sleep; And the sen - tries watch the sen - tries watch Till

The Girls At Home 3

gleams be - yond the foam, So a light springs up in the

love of which they roam; But the fi - nal song and the

morn - ing gilds the dome; Till the rat - tling drum shall the

Sol - dier's heart, As he thinks of the Girls at Home.

sweet - est one, Is the song of the Girls at Home.

sleep - ers rouse From their dream of the Girls at Home.

COMPOSITIONS

OF

Henry C. Work.

BALLADS.

Days when we were young	30
First Love Dream	30
Our Captain's Last Words	30

SONGS & CHORUSES.

Agnes by the River	30
Andy Veto	30
Babylon is Fallen	30
Beautiful Rose	30
Buckskin Bag of Gold	35
Columbia's Guardian Ang ls	30
Come back to the Farm	30
Come Home Father	30
Corporal Schnapps	30
Grafted into the Army	30
Grandmother told me so	30
Kingdom Coming	30
Lillie of the Snow Storm	30
Little Major	30
Marching through Georgia	30
Nellie Lost and Found	30
Now Moses	30
No Letters from Home	35

Our last grand Camping Ground	30
Picture on the Wall	30
Ring the Bell, Watchman	25
Ship that never returned	30
Sleeping for the Flag	30
Song of a thousand Years	30
Song of the Red Man	35
'Tis Finished	30
Uncle Joe's Hail Columbia	30
Wake Nicodemus,	35
Wake the Boys to search for Nellie	30
Washington and Lincoln	30
Watching for Pa	30
We'll go down Ourselves	30
Who shall Rule this American Nation	30
When the Evening Star went down	30

DUETS.

Sleep Baby, Sleep	30

QUARTETS.

Crossing the Grand Sierras	75
Girls at Home	30
God save the Nation	25
Poor Kitty Pop Corn	35

CLEVELAND:

Published by S. BRAINARD'S SONS, 203 Superior St.

Grafted Into The Army

Words and Music by HENRY C. WORK
Nº 13

1. Our Jim-my has gone for to   live in a tent,   They have graft-ed him in-to the

2. Drest   up in his u - ni corn__ dear lit - tle chap;   They have graft-ed him in-to the

3. Now   in my pro-vis-ions I   see him re-vealed__ They have graft-ed him in-to the

ar - my; He fin - al - ly puck - er'd up cour - age and went, When they
ar - my; It seems but a day since he sot in my lap, But they
ar - my; A pick - et be - side the con - tent - ed field, They have

graft - ed him in - to the ar - my. I told them the child was too
graft - ed him in - to the ar - my. And these are the trou - sies he
graft - ed him in - to the ar - my. He looks kind - er sick - ish be -

young, a - las! At the cap - tain's fore - quar - ters, they said he would pass__ They'd
used to wear__ Them ver - y same but - tons__ the patch and the tear__ But
gins to cry__ A big vol - un - teer stand - ing right in his eye! Oh

train him up well in the in - fan - try class__ So they grafted him in - to the ar - my.
Un - cle Sam gave him a bran new pair When they grafted him in - to the ar - my.
what if the duck - y should up and die Now they've grafted him in - to the ar - my.

Grafted Into 3

AIR

ALTO

TENOR

BASS

Oh Jim - my, far - well! Your broth - ers fell Way

Oh Jim - my, far - well! Your broth - ers fell Way

down in Al - a - bar - my; I thought they would spare a

down in Al - a - bar - my; I thought they would spare a

lone wid-der's heir, But they graft - ed him in - to the ar - my.

lone wid-der's heir, But they graft - ed him in - to the ar - my.

Grafted Into 3

DAD'S

–A–

MILLIONAIRE!

Song and Chorus.

WORDS AND MUSIC BY

HENRY CLAY WORK.

CLEVELAND: –3–

Published by S. BRAINARD'S SONS, 203 Superior St.

Dad's A Millionaire

Words and Music by HENRY C. WORK
Nº 39

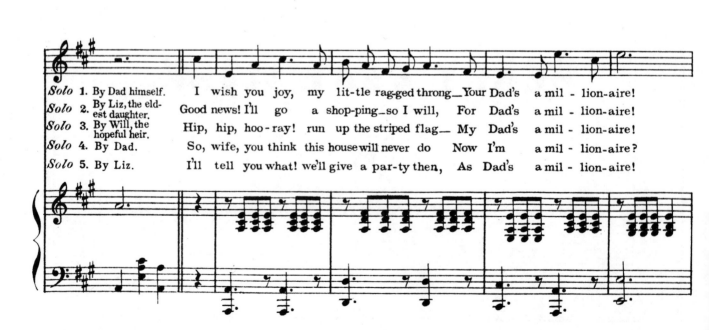

Solo 1. By Dad himself.   I wish you joy, my lit-tle rag-ged throng___Your Dad's   a mil - lion-aire!

Solo 2. By Liz, the eld-est daughter.   Good news! I'll   go   a shop-ping___so I will,   For   Dad's   a mil - lion-aire!

Solo 3. By Will, the hopeful heir.   Hip, hip, hoo-ray! run   up the striped flag___ My   Dad's   a mil - lion-aire!

Solo 4. By Dad.   So, wife, you think this house will never do   Now I'm   a mil - lion-aire?

Solo 5. By Liz.   I'll   tell   you what! we'll give a par-ty then,   As Dad's   a mil - lion-aire!

The for-tune's come, we've wait-ed for so long, And I'm a mil - lion-aire! Come
And I must have a thousand dol-lar bill, As Dad's a mil - lion-aire! Put
This bless-ed day, I'll buy a trot-ting nag, For Dad's a mil - lion-aire! I
Well, I must build a mansion then for you, As I'm a mil - lion-aire! Though
And we'll in-vite none but the "up-per ten," Since Dad's a mil - lion-aire! I

Will, come Bub— go buy some better shoes; Come Liz, come Lu— go tell your Ma the news—
on your duds, and you'll go with me Lu! Come Bub, go call a car-riage from the square;
vow, I'll smoke three-cent ci-gars no more! Here, take them Bub, and pitch them out the door;
as for me, I think I should in-vest— My whole pile in some mammoth farm out West,
should be sure to find an-oth-er beau, For dukes and lords, and no-bles would be there—

Though once so poor, we're now as rich as Jews, For I'm a mil - lion-aire.
We'll ride in style a-long the av-e-nue, For Dad's a mil - lion-aire.
I'll have the best— the dear-est in the store, Now Dad's a mil - lion-aire.
Yet I can build, if you should think it best, Since I'm a mil - lion-aire.
I've turn'd him off— the tai-lor's clerk, you know, Now Dad's a mil - lion-aire.

3 times
Back to
Verse

no
chorus

Dad's A 3

Chorus *With spirit*

AIR

Hur - rah! hur-rah! now give us a rous-ing song—Good bye! good bye! to poverty, want and care;

ALTO

Hur - rah! hur-rah! now give us a rous-ing song—Good bye! good bye! to poverty, want and care;

TENOR

Hur - rah! hur-rah! now give us a rous-ing song—Good bye! good bye! to poverty, want and care;

BASS

The for-tune's come, we've wait-ed for so long, And Dad's a mil - lion-aire!

The for-tune's come, we've wait-ed for so long, And Dad's a mil - lion-aire!

The for-tune's come, we've wait-ed for so long, And Dad's a mil - lion-aire!

COMPOSITIONS

OF

Henry C. Work.

CLEVELAND:

Published by S. BRAINARD'S SONS, 203 Superior St.

Entered according to Act of Congress, A. D. 186 by ROOT & CADY, in the Office of the Librarian of Congress, at Washington.

Crossing The

Grand Sierras

Words and Music by HENRY C. WORK
Nº 46

148

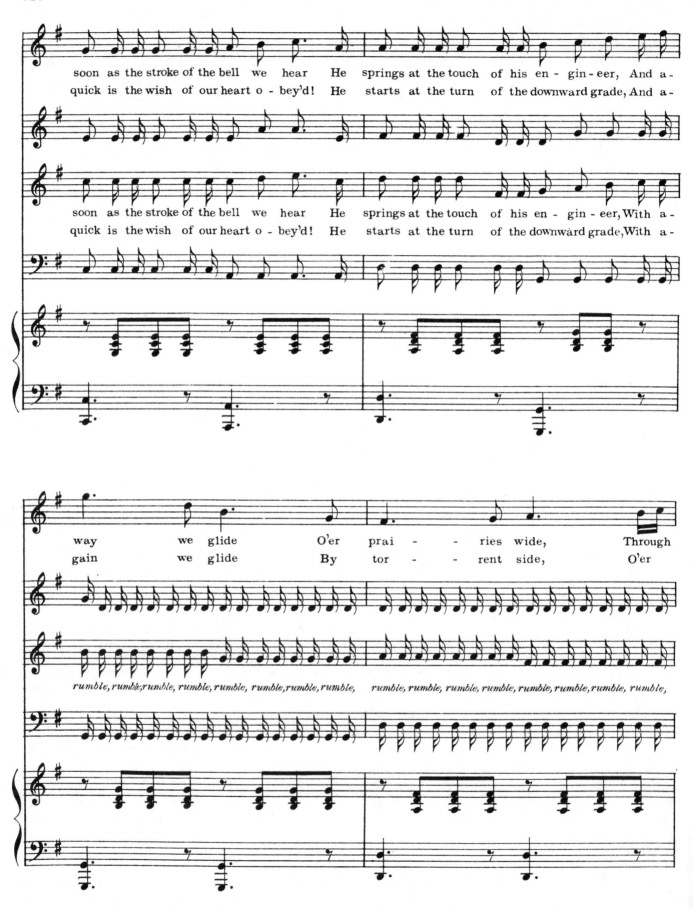

soon as the stroke of the bell we hear He springs at the touch of his en - gin - eer, And a -
quick is the wish of our heart o - bey'd! He starts at the turn of the downward grade, And a -

soon as the stroke of the bell we hear He springs at the touch of his en - gin - eer, With a -
quick is the wish of our heart o - bey'd! He starts at the turn of the downward grade, With a -

way we glide O'er prai - - ries wide, Through
gain we glide By tor - - rent side, O'er

rumble, rumble, rumble, rumble, rumble, rumble, rumble, rumble, *rumble, rumble, rumble, rumble, rumble, rumble, rumble, rumble,*

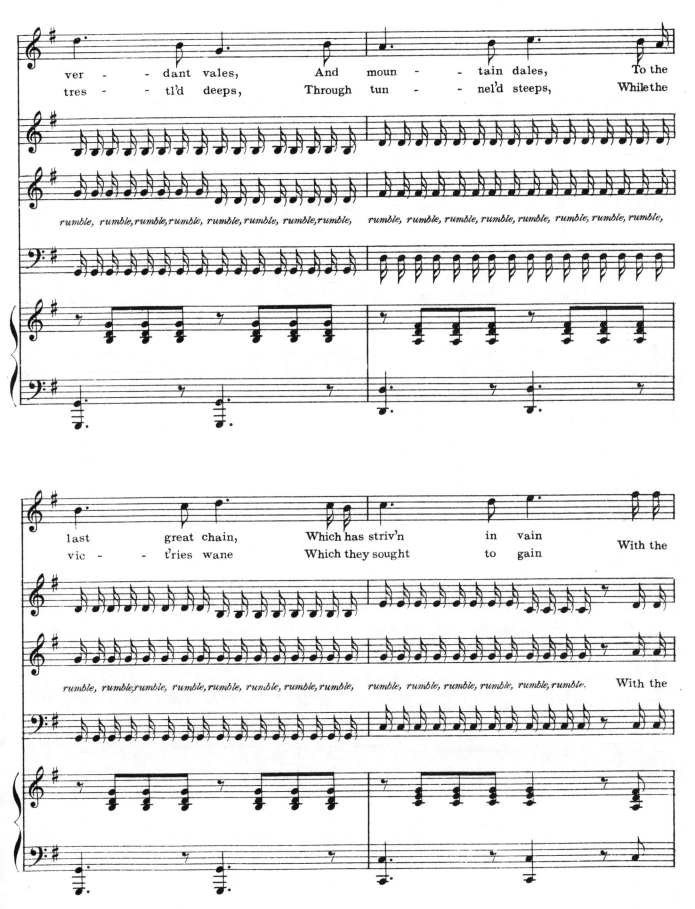

last   great chain,   Which has striv'n   in vain   To the
vic - - t'ries wane   Which they sought   to gain   While the

Light - ning! the Light - ning! the Light - ning Pal - ace Train.

Light - ning! the Light - ning! the Light - ning Pal - ace Train.

Duet

AIR

1. For - get - ting far At - lan - tic, And mid - way scenes ro - man - tic, We
2. 'Neath tim - ber'd roofs un - end - ing, From win - ter snows de - fend - ing, Through

ALTO

scale the peaks gi - gan - tic, Which guard the Land of Gold:
can - yons wild des - cend - ing To the City of the Plain:

Her sil - ver rills are leap - ing, Her love - ly lakes are sleep - ing And
We leave the scenes ter - rif - ic, We pass the fields pro - lif - ic, And

snow clad gran - ites keep - ing Their "watch of years" un - told.
view the broad Pa - cif - ic The Gold - en gat - ed main.

Chorus

sing it on the plain! We've climb'd the Grand Si - er - ras With the

sing it on the plain! We've climb'd the Grand Si - er - ras With the

Lightning Palace Train, With the Light ning! the Lightning! the Lightning Palace Train.

Lightning Palace Train, With the Light ning! the Lightning! the Lightning Palace Train.

Poor Kitty Popcorn

OR THE

SOLDIER'S PET.

WORDS AND MUSIC BY

HENRY C. WORK.

CLEVELAND:

Published by S BRAINARD'S SONS, 203 Superior St.

Poor Kitty Popcorn,

OR THE

Soldier's Pet

Words and Music by HENRY C. WORK
Nº 34

First verse, rapidly — second, lively — third, moderately — fourth, slowly.

1. Did you ev-er hear the sto-ry of the loy-al cat? *Me - yow!* _____ Who was

2. Round her neck she wore a rib-bon _ she was black as jet _ *Me - yow!* _____ And at

3. Now the "cru-el war is o-ver" and the troops dis-band _ *Me - yow!* _____ Kit-ty

4. So she wan-ders on the prairie till she sees his form _ *Me - yow!* _____ Carried

troops came nigh, And she fell in-to the col-umn with a low glad cry, Me - yow!___

feet were sore, Whisp'ring in his ear with wonder at the can - non's roar, Me yow!___

dim blue eyes, Till by strangers driven rude-ly from the door she cries, Me - yow!___

snow falls fast, And a - lone a-mid the darkness there she breathes her last Me yow!___

Chorus

AIR

Poor Kit-ty Pop-corn! Bur-ied in a snow-drift now___ Nev-er

ALTO

Poor Kit-ty Pop-corn! Bur-ied in a snow-drift now___ Nev-er

TENOR

Poor Kit-ty Pop-corn! Bur-ied in a snow-drift now___ Nev-er

BASS

COMPOSITIONS

OF

Henry C. Work.

BALLADS.

Days when we were young	30
First Love Dream	30
Our Captain's Last Words	30

SONGS & CHORUSES.

Agnes by the River	30
Andy Veto	30
Babylon is Fallen	30
Beautiful Rose	30
Buckskin Bag of Gold	35
Columbia's Guardian Angels	30
Come back to the Farm	30
Come Home Father	30
Corporal Schnapps	30
Grafted into the Army	30
Grandmother told me so	30
Kingdom Coming	30
Lillie of the Snow Storm	30
Little Major	30
Marching through Georgia	30
Nellie Lost and Found	30
Now Moses	30
No Letters from Home	35

Our last grand Camping Ground	30
Picture on the Wall	30
Ring the Bell, Watchman	25
Ship that never returned	30
Sleeping for the Flag	30
Song of a thousand Years	30
Song of the Red Man	35
'Tis Finished	30
Uncle Joe's Hail Columbia	30
Wake Nicodemus,	35
Wake the Boys to search for Nellie	30
Washington and Lincoln	30
Watching for Pa	30
We'll go down Ourselves	30
Who shall Rule this American Nation	30
When the Evening Star went down	30

DUETS.

Sleep Baby, Sleep	30

QUARTETS.

Crossing the Grand Sierras	75
Girls at Home	30
God save the Nation	25
Poor Kitty Pop Corn	35

CLEVELAND:

Published by S. BRAINARD'S SONS, 203 Superior St.

Entered according to Act of Congress, A. D. 186 by ROOT & CADY, in the Office of the Librarian of Congress, at Washington.

Kingdom Coming

Words and Music by HENRY C. WORK
Nº 10

1. Say, dar-keys, hab you seen de mas-sa, Wid de muff-stash on his face, Go long de road some time dis morn-in', Like he gwine to leab de place? He seen a smoke, way up de rib-ber, Whar de Link-um gum-boats lay; He took his hat, an' lef berry sudden An' I

Chorus

Second Verse

He six foot one way, two feet tud-der, An' he weigh tree hun-dred pound, His
coat so big, he couldn't pay de tail-or, An' it won't go half way round. He
drill so much dey call him Cap-'an, An' he get so dref-ful tann'd, I
spec he try an' fool dem Yan-kees For to tink he's con - tra - band.

CHORUS.

Third Verse

De dar-keys feel so lone-some lib-ing in de log-house on de lawn, Dey
move dar tings to mas-sa's par-lor For to keep it while he's gone. Dar's
wine an' ci - der in de kit-chen, An' de dar-keys dey'll hab some; I
spose dey'll all be corn - fis - ca-ted When de Lin - kum so - jers come.

CHORUS.

Fourth Verse

De o - ber-seer he make us trou-ble, An' he dribe us round a spell; We
lock him up in de smoke house cel - lar, Wid de key trown in de well. De
whip is lost, de han' - cuff bro-ken, But de mas - sa'll hab his pay; He's
ole e-nough, big e-nough, ought to known bet - ter Dan to went an' run a - way.

CHORUS.

Kingdom Coming 3

SONG AND CHORUS

WORDS AND MUSIC BY

HENRY C. WORK.

NEW YORK:
Published by C. M. CADY, 107 Duane St.

To my sister Louisa

The Mystic Veil

Words and Music by HENRY C. WORK.
Nº 50

When the shadows take their nightly pla - ces,   When de-parting light is faint and pale,   Then
When my song, in lonely notes as - cend - ing,   Vain-ly bids my sadden'd soul re-join,   Me -
Wak-ing while the denser darkness lin - gers,   Some one seems to stand beside my bed;   I

in my chamber gather phantom fa - ces, Gaz - ing thro' the mys - tic veil.
thinks I hear a murmur'd al - to blend - ing: Is it real - ly your sweet voice?
can but think I feel your fair - y fin - gers, Soft - ly laid up - on my head.

One there is with features so fa - mil - iar, Glimpse of her give my pulse a start; Oh!
An - swer now, if on - ly by a whis - per; Rend the veil, the mystic veil, a - part: And
Si - lent - ly why does the vis - ion van - ish? Dream I yet, or is it ma - gic art? Now

tell me tell me true - ly is it you, love, Come to cheer my lone - ly heart?
tell me tell me true - ly is it you, love, Come to cheer my lone - ly heart?
tell me tell me true - ly is it you, love, Come to cheer my lone - ly heart?

168

Chorus

The Mystic Veil 3

COMPOSITIONS

OF

Henry C. Work.

CLEVELAND:

Published by S. BRAINARD'S SONS, 203 Superior St.

Song Of A Thousand Years

HENRY C. WORK

Maestoso

1. Lift up your eyes de-spond-ing free-men! Fling to the winds your need-less
2. What if the clouds, one lit-tle mo-ment, Hide the blue sky where morn ap-
3. Tell the great world these bless-ed tid-ings! Yes, and be sure the bond-man

fears! He who un-furl'd your beauteous ban-ner, Says it shall wave a thou-sand years!
pears, When the bright sun, that tints them crimson, Ri-ses to shine a thou-sand years!
hears; Tell the op-press'd of ev'-ry na-tion, Ju-bi-lee lasts a thou-sand years!

Chorus

"A thou-sand years!" my own Co - lum - bi - a! 'Tis the glad day so long fore-

"A thou-sand years!" my own Co - lum - bi - a! 'Tis the glad day so long fore-

told! 'Tis the glad morn whose ear-ly twi-light Washington saw in times of old.

told! 'Tis the glad morn whose ear-ly twi-light Washington saw in times of old.

4. Envious foes, beyond the ocean!
Little we heed your threat'ning sneers;
Little will they— our children's children—
When you are gone a thousand years.

5. Rebels at home! go hide your faces—
Weep for your crimes with bitter tears;
You could not bind the blessed daylight,
Though you should strive a thousand years.

6. Back to your dens, ye secret traitors!
Down to your own degraded spheres!
Ere the first blaze of dazzling sunshine
Shortens your lives a thousand years.

7. Haste thee along, thou glorious Noonday!
Oh, for the eyes of ancient seers!
Oh, for the faith of Him who reckons
Each of his days a thousand years!

Song ƒ A Thousand Years 2

And the towering granite crest
Nobly guards his place of rest,
Near the lovely lake of

SWEET ECHO DELL

Song and Chorus.

WORDS AND MUSIC BY

HENRY C. WORK.

NEW YORK:

Published by C. M. CADY, 107 Duane St.

To my Sister Etta

Sweet Echo Dell

*Three sons of a New England widow had long toiled in the Land of Gold, when this message reached them:
"Come and see your mother before she dies!" They started immediately, but while crossing the Sierra Nevada
the youngest became ill, and in a few hours breathed his last. He was buried in a lovely spot, near the
summit. The mother lived long enough to greet her surviving sons; but her mind wandered, and she never
fully realized that Willie had gone before.*

Words and Music by HENRY C. WORK
Nº 51

1. Three there
2. Is he
3. Com ing

were that left my cot; Two are here, and one is not; Why does
la - den well with gold? Does he bring me wealth un - told? Why then
homeward, does he sing Like a lark up - on the wing? Why then

Wil - lie lin - ger? Say, can you tell?" "He was wea - ry by the way; When we
does he lin - ger? Say, can you tell? "All his treasures are a - bove; All he
does he lin - ger? Say, can you tell? Naught is heard but rippling waves, War-bling

came he could but stay In the sha - dy grove at Sweet Ech - o Dell."
sent you was his love, With a whispered prayer from Sweet Ech - o Dell."
birds, and shouting braves; Si - lent is his voice in Sweet Ech - o Dell."

Chorus

AIR *mf*

Ech - o Dell! Ech - o Dell! It was

ALTO *pp* *p*

TENOR *pp* *p*

Ech - o Dell! Ech - o Dell! It was

BASS *pp* *p*

there we soft-ly said "Fare - well!"   And the   towering granite crest   No - bly

Farewell!"

there we soft-ly said "Fare - well!"   And the   towering granite crest   No - bly

guards his place of   rest,   Near the   love-ly lake of Sweet   Ech-o   Dell.

guards his place of   rest,   Near the   love-ly lake of Sweet   Ech-o   Dell.

4.   Is he coming by-and-by?
      May I bless him ere I die?
  Why then does he linger? Say, can you tell?"
      Mirrored in that mountain lake,
      Heaven is near, and he will wake
  Never elsewhere than in Sweet Echo Dell."
                                    Chorus.

5.   Would you crush my only joy?
      Surely I shall meet my boy;
  Why then does he linger? Say, can you tell?"
      Never will his weary feet
      Travel more, yet may you meet
  When your soul floats over Sweet Echo Dell."
                                    Chorus.

Sweet Echo Dell 3

GRAND-FATHER'S CLOCK.

Song and Chorus.

WORDS AND MUSIC BY

HENRY C. WORK.

NEW YORK:

Published by C. M. CADY, 107 Duane St.

To my Sister Lizzie

Grandfather's Clock

Words and Music by HENRY C. WORK
Nº 52

1. My grand-father's clock was too large for the shelf, So it stood ninety years on the floor; It was

2. In watch- ing its pen - du-lum swing to and fro, Ma-ny hours had he spent while a boy; And in

3. My grandfa-ther said that of those he could hire, Not a ser-vant so faith-ful he found; For it

4. It rang an a-larm in the dead of the night_An a - larm that for years had been dumb; And we

tall-er by half than the old man himself, Though it weighed not a pen-ny weight more. It was
childhood and man-hood the clock seemed to know And to share both his grief and his joy. For it
wast-ed no time, and had but one de-sire—At the close of each week to be wound. And it
knew that his spir-it was plum-ing for flight—That his hour of de-parture had come. Still the

bought on the morn of the day that he was born, And was al-ways his treasure and pride; But it
struck twenty-four when he en-tered at the door, With a blooming and beau-ti-ful bride; But it
kept in its place—not a frown up-on its face, And its hands nev-er hung by its side; But it
clock kept the time, with a soft and muffled chime, As we si-lent-ly stood by-his side; But it

stopp'd short nev-er to go a-gain When the old man died.
stopp'd short nev-er to go a-gain When the old man died.
stopp'd short nev-er to go a-gain When the old man died.
stopp'd short nev-er to go a-gain When the old man died.

Grandfathers Clock 3

180

Chorus